Steven

QUIZ
FACTS
EARTH
& SPACE

Kingfisher Books, Grisewood & Dempsey Ltd,
Elsley House, 24–30 Great Titchfield Street, London W1P 7AD

First published in 1993 by Kingfisher Books
10 9 8 7 6 5 4 3

Some of the material in this edition was previously published by Kingfisher Books in
*Question & Answer Encyclopedia: Why Is It?, How Does It Work?, What Is It?,
Where Is It?, When Did It Happen?*

British Library Cataloguing-in-Publication Data
A catalogue record for this book is available from the British Library

ISBN 0 86272 992 0

Edited by Cynthia O'Neill
Designed and typeset by Talkback International Limited
Printed by BPCC Hazell Books Ltd, Aylesbury, Buckinghamshire

QUIZ FACTS
EARTH
& SPACE

**Quiz Questions by
George Beal**

Kingfisher Books

EARTH & SPACE

WHEN DID THE OLD AND NEW WORLDS SEPARATE?

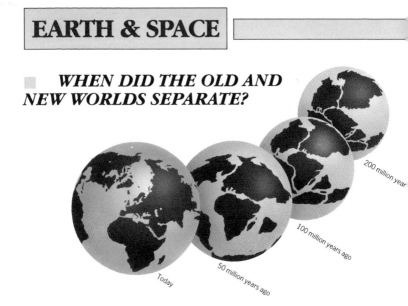

200 million year

100 million years ago

50 million years ago

Today

The continents of the Old World (Europe, Asia and Africa) and the New World (The Americas) have been slowly drifting on the surface of the Earth since our planet became solid. In the last 150 million years, the Atlantic has gradually opened up, separating the Americas from Africa and Europe.

Alaska and Siberia were once joined, but at present Alaska and Siberia are separated by the Bering Strait.

QUIZ 1

1 What are the 'monuments' on the Colorado Plateau?

2 Are these monuments naturally formed?

3 Is it possible to find snow at the Equator?

4 Do Equatorial mountains always have snow?

5 Name an Equatorial mountain with snow.

6 How high is Mount Kilimanjaro?

7 Is the Earth a perfect sphere?

8 Is the Equator a perfect circle?

9 What is the circumference of the Earth at the Equator?

10 What is the Earth's diameter at the Equator?

WHEN DID THE ALPS FORM?

The Alps are made mainly of rock layers which were uplifted and folded about 25 million years ago.

The Alps are part of a series of fold mountains stretching through Europe and the Middle East to the Himalayas and other mountains of Asia. They are the result of the movement of continents since the break-up of the supercontinent Pangaea. Africa and Eurasia drifted eastwards and rotated towards each other. Sediments in the ocean floor between these continents were compressed, folded and uplifted.

WHEN DID SEA CHARTS COME INTO USE?

The earliest record of a sea chart dates from 1270 when Louis IX of France studied a chart on board a

Genoese ship during the Eighth Crusade. The earliest navigators kept close to land or drifted with ocean currents.

Once the compass was used, ships could sail more directly from one port to another. The Chinese and Arabs may have used sea-charts before Europeans, but none survive. From about 1200, compasses and rudders were used on European ships. Navigators used *portolani,* books which listed ports, landmarks, distances and navigational advice.

WHEN WERE THE FIRST MAPS MADE?

Simple sketch-maps were probably drawn before people could write, so maps may be older than written history. The oldest surviving map was drawn on a Babylonian tablet about 2300 BC.

An ancient map was found at Gar-Sur, nearly 400 kilometres north of Babylon. It shows mountains and a river (probably the Euphrates) flowing through a delta. Scientific mapmaking began with the Greeks.

QUIZ 2

1 Name three fossil fuels.

2 What did oil and gas form from?

3 What name do we give rocks which allow liquids through?

4 What name do we give rocks which don't allow liquids through?

5 When was coal formed?

6 From what was coal formed?

7 What is a 'seam' of coal?

8 How old are the oldest coal seams?

9 Where is the deepest coal shaft in the world?

WHY DID DINOSAURS DIE OUT SO SUDDENLY?

Dinosaurs became extinct about 65 million years ago, at the end of Cretaceous times. They had existed for 130 million years. No one knows why they died out.

Many other types of animals died out at the same time as the dinosaurs, including flying and sea reptiles. But a few reptiles did survive, including turtles, lizards and snakes. There are many theories to explain why the dinosaurs died out, including changes of climate and vegetation, cold winters, new parasites and diseases.

WHY ARE FOSSILS IMPORTANT TO GEOLOGISTS?

Fossils help geologists to put different kinds of rocks in the same age-group. Fossils also give information about the conditions that existed when they were alive. And similar fossils in different places help in the study of continental drift.

The most useful fossils are of plants and animals which lived in a wide variety of places, but only for a short period of time. These are called index fossils.

QUIZ 3

1 What is the inside of the Earth like?

2 What are the layers inside the Earth called?

3 What is seismology?

4 How many different kinds of earthquake waves are there?

5 What are the different kinds of earthquake wave?

6 Which earthquake waves travel fastest?

7 Where was the worst earthquake this century?

8 How many died?

9 What does the Richter Scale measure?

10 What does a high number on the Richter scale show?

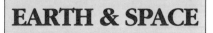

QUIZ 4

1 What is geodesy?

2 What are geodimeters used for?

3 What did Eratosthenes do in 250 BC?

4 Who was James Hutton?

5 What are the three main groups of rocks?

6 What does the word 'igneous' mean?

7 What were igneous rocks made from?

8 What are sedimentary rocks?

9 What does the word 'metamorphic' mean?

WHY ARE THERE COAL SEAMS IN THE ANTARCTIC?

Coal is a rock made of the fossil remains of plants. The icy Antarctic has very few plants now; however, when these coal seams were formed, there must have been plenty of plants, and the climate must have been warmer.

The coal seams of the Antarctic were formed about 250 million years ago when Antarctica was part of the supercontinent, Pangaea.

500 million years ago

WHY DO THE CONTINENTS MOVE ABOUT?

The crust of the Earth is a relatively thin layer. Scientists believe it is divided into huge sections called 'plates'. These are moved very slowly by convection currents inside the Earth.

325 million years ago

The scientist Alfred Wegener suggested in 1915 that the continents might have moved. He had noticed that their shapes fit together like a jigsaw. His theory was called 'continental drift'.

175 million years ago

50 million years ago

WHY DO VOLCANOES ERUPT?

Ash

Lava

Rising magma

The lava of volcanoes is molten rock, called magma. Some magma rises straight from the Earth's mantle to the surface. Some is stored in a magma chamber in the crust, where the gases collect and help to drive the magma out.

The upper part of the mantle, under the Earth's crust, is nearly molten. Magma contains several gases, and bubbles of this expand near the surface and drive the magma out as an eruption. Volcanic eruptions vary from place to place, mainly according to how fluid or gaseous the lava is.

WHERE DO GEYSERS OCCUR?

All geysers occur in areas of volcanic activity, but not all volcanic areas have geysers. They only occur where water can soak through cracks in the rocks and collect underground.

QUIZ 5

1 *What would happen if the planets revolved too quickly?*

2 *Which planet spins faster – Venus or Pluto?*

3 *In which direction does Jupiter spin?*

4 *In which direction do most of the planets revolve around the Sun?*

5 *Is the Solar System at the centre of the Universe?*

6 *What does a cell need to survive?*

7 *Do water and oxygen exist on other planets?*

8 *Why is the ozone in the atmosphere important for life?*

Here the water is heated under pressure, and as it starts to bubble out there is a sudden gush of steam and hot water high into the air.

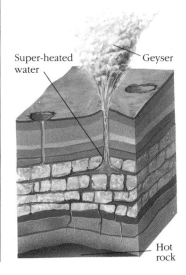

Super-heated water

Geyser

Hot rock

▪ WHY DO EARTHQUAKES OCCUR ONLY IN SOME PARTS OF THE WORLD?

The map shows where earthquakes have happened. These occur near the edges of the Earth's crustal plates.

The plates are slowly moving together or apart. For instance, one zone encircles the Pacific. Here, the floor of the Pacific is being pushed down under the continents, and this gradual movement of Pacific plates against the continental plates causes earthquakes. Other zones are in the Mediterranean and the Atlantic.

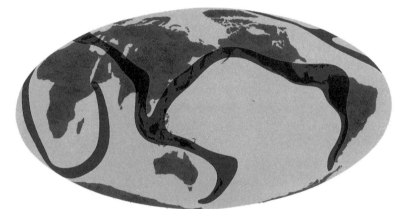

▪ WHY DOES IT GET COLDER AS YOU CLIMB A MOUNTAIN?

As you climb up a high mountain the air gets colder. You may be a kilometre nearer the Sun, but the Sun is still 150 million kilometres away!

The Sun heats the Earth, and it is the Earth that heats the air. The Sun's energy arrives as shortwave radiation, which is easily absorbed by the air. There is more air to absorb the heat near the Earth's surface than higher up. So the higher you go, the colder it gets.

QUIZ 6

1 How far is the nearest star?
2 Could we see a planet near a star at that distance?
3 At what speed does light travel?
4 How many kilometres are there in a light year?
5 Do we know if planets exist in any other Solar Systems?
6 What is the name of the star nearest to our Sun?
7 Which star is brightest in the sky?
8 What term is applied to the feeling of weightlessness while falling?
9 Where does an astronaut float?
10 Around which does a planet revolve - a star or a moon?

EARTH & SPACE

WHY IS SEA WATER SALTY?

Sea water contains many minerals. They have all been washed out of the land and carried to the sea by rivers or glaciers. When sea water evaporates, these minerals remain in the sea and become more concentrated. This makes the water salty. The saltiest sea of all is the Dead Sea.

Salt (sodium chloride) makes up about 85 per cent of all the minerals in sea water. The saltiness of deep-sea water is fairly constant, but near the surface it varies from place to place. It is low where lots of fresh water is added from rivers.

QUIZ 7

1 What is a planet?

2 If a planet is a dark body, how can it be seen?

3 What is a moon?

4 How many planets are there?

5 Which planets do not have satellites?

6 How many moons has Jupiter?

7 What names are given to the moons of Mars?

8 Which is the biggest satellite in the Solar System?

9 Of which planet is Titan a satellite?

10 Can we see Jupiter's big satellite?

WHY DO THE TIDES RISE AND FALL?

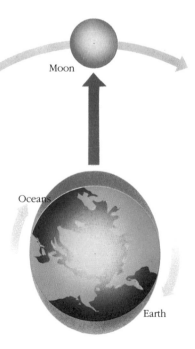

Moon

Oceans

Earth

The water in the oceans is held close to the Earth by gravity. But the Moon and Sun also have some 'pull' on the Earth. The Moon's gravity affects water in the oceans. The sea is 'pulled' slightly towards the Moon, causing a bulge, or high tide. On the opposite side, the sea is pushed away, causing a second bulge.

High tides occur twice in about 25 hours. This is because at the same time as the Earth is rotating on its axis, the Moon is travelling round the Earth (every 27 days).

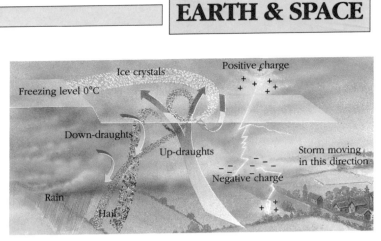

Ice crystals
Positive charge
Freezing level 0°C
Down-draughts
Up-draughts
Storm moving in this direction
Negative charge
Rain
Hail

WHY DO CLOUDS FORM?

A cloud is made up of tiny droplets of water or ice. When cloud forms, the invisible water vapour in the air condenses into visible droplets of water.

All air contains water vapour. Warm air can hold more water vapour than cold air. If the air cools down, it cannot hold so much water vapour, and it turns into tiny droplets of water. Air cools down when it rises, because the higher in the atmosphere it goes, the cooler it gets. When it rains, the tiny droplets in a cloud form bigger drops which fall to Earth.

WHY DOES THUNDER FOLLOW LIGHTNING?

Lightning is a huge spark of electricity. Thunder is the sound the air makes as it is suddenly heated up by lightning. They both happen at the same time, but as light travels faster than sound, we see the lightning first and then hear the thunder.

Thunder is caused when lightning heats up the molecules of air along its path. The heated molecules expand, collide with cooler molecules and set up sound waves. Light travels very quickly, at about 300,000 kilometres per second. Sound is slower, travelling at about 20 kilometres per minute.

QUIZ 8

1 What is the time between New and Full Moon called?
2 What happens when the Moon wanes?
3 Does the Moon have an atmosphere?
4 How old is the Moon believed to be?
5 How long does the Moon's cycle of phases last?
6 How were lunar craters formed?
7 Why do the craters show so clearly on the Moon?
8 Did the Earth ever have craters like the Moon?
9 In Roman mythology, who was the goddess of the Moon?

WHAT IS THE ATMOSPHERE MADE OF?

The atmosphere is the air which surrounds the planet Earth. The gases in the air allow plants, animals and humans to live. The dampness and movement of the air near the Earth causes our weather. The atmosphere also shields us from the Sun's harmful rays and from falling meteorites.

Air is made up of many gases. The most common are nitrogen (78%) and oxygen (21%).

There are small amounts of other gases, including argon, water vapour and carbon dioxide.

WHAT IS HAIL?

Hail is made up of layers of ice. This is because a hailstone has risen high into the coldest part of a storm cloud again and again.

Each time it rises, another layer of ice freezes around it until the hailstone is so heavy that it falls to Earth. For a hailstorm to occur the top of the cloud must be colder than freezing level.

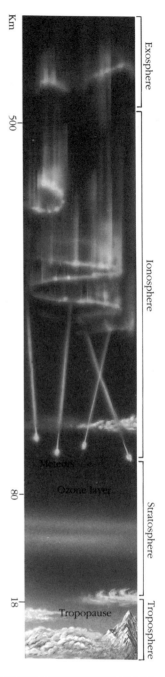

Km — Exosphere — 500 — Ionosphere — Meteors — 80 — Ozone layer — Stratosphere — 18 — Tropopause — Troposphere

QUIZ 9

1 Which way is the night hemisphere of the Moon turned?

2 How many days after a New Moon might a crescent Moon be seen?

3 Why can't we see a true New Moon?

4 How far is the Moon from the Earth?

5 Is there any life on the Moon?

6 Why is there no noise on the Moon?

7 What is the temperature of the Moon at midday?

8 Is there life on Mars?

9 Who wrote War of the Worlds about a Martian invasion?

WHAT KINDS OF CLOUDS CAN WE SEE?

Clouds are made of millions of tiny water droplets or ice crystals suspended in the air. They are named according to their shape and height.

Cirrostratus is a thin, almost transparent layer of cloud at a high level. Altostratus is a thicker layer of cloud at a higher level. Nimbostratus forms at a lower level, while stratus clouds are layers within 500 metres of the Earth's surface. 'Puffy' clouds, known as cumulus clouds, are called altocumulus at a high level. When they join together they form stratocumulus. Cumulonimbus are towering thunder clouds. A third type of cloud is cirrus, wisps of cloud high in the sky.

QUIZ 10

1 Which is the 'Red Planet'?
2 What element do the rocks on Mars contain?
3 What is the dusty material which covers Mars?
4 Why is the sky of Mars pink?
5 Why does the surface of Mars disappear from our sight?
6 Name a place where 'rusty' rocks might be found on Earth.
7 Which is the largest planet?
8 How fast does Jupiter spin?
9 How fast does Saturn spin?
10 If it did not rotate, what shape would Jupiter be?

WHY DO TREES GET STRUCK BY LIGHTNING?

When lightning flashes from a cloud to Earth, it takes the easiest path. It is attracted to the highest point in the area, and this is often a damp tree.

A lightning flash begins with a downward 'leader stroke'. Air is very resistant to electricity, and the leader stroke is attracted to trees and high buildings. A tree offers a low-resistance route to Earth. Tall buildings also attract lightning.

WHY DO SOME RIVERS HAVE DELTAS?

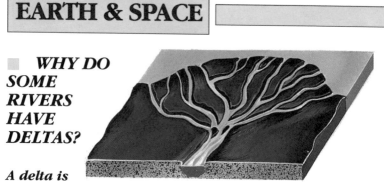

A delta is shaped like a triangle, which is also the shape of the Greek letter D, called 'Delta'. A river delta is caused by deposits at the mouth of the river. This happens when the river transports more silt to its mouth than can be removed by currents or tides.

The Mediterranean Sea has a very small tidal range, so big rivers like the Nile and the Rhône have very big deltas. Deltas are less common on rivers that flow to oceans and tidal seas.

QUIZ 11

1 Of what acid do the clouds on Venus consist?

2 How long is a 'day' on Venus?

3 Is there much cloud on Venus?

4 How hot is Venus at midday?

5 How far is Venus from the Sun?

6 Which planet is nearest to the Sun?

7 How long is a 'year' on Mercury?

8 How many kilometres across does Mercury measure?

9 How many moons does Mercury have?

10 Can we see Mercury from Earth?

WHY DO LAKES SOMETIMES DISAPPEAR?

Many lakes have vanished. Some have been filled up, the water of others has flowed away, and other lakes in very hot countries have simply dried up.

Lakes can be filled up with material brought down by rivers. Deltas in a lake can eventually fill up the whole lake, which becomes an almost flat plain. Some lakes dry up because of evaporation, and some disappear and return, such as Lake Eyre in Australia. It is a huge lake, but it disappears in dry weather.

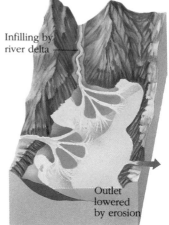

Infilling by river delta

Outlet lowered by erosion

WHY DO GLACIERS APPEAR?

A glacier is like a great river of ice. Glaciers appear when more snow falls than melts every year. The snow collects, squeezing the lower layer hard. It turns to ice and forms a glacier.

All the time snow is being added at the top, the glacier will move forward under its own weight. Most glaciers today are left over from the last Ice Age. In the past two million years there have been five glaciations.

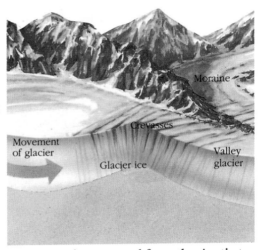

Ice-sheets spread from mountain areas and from the Arctic to cover most of Europe.

QUIZ 12

1 What are Saturn's rings made of?

2 Who discovered Saturn's rings?

3 How big are the rings?

4 How thick are the rings?

5 How were the Sun and planets formed?

6 When were the Sun and planets formed?

7 Does Jupiter have a strong gravitational pull?

8 What makes up 90 per cent of the giant planets?

9 Where would you see the Great Red Spot?

WHY DO WE SEE RAINBOWS?

When sunlight passes through raindrops it is slightly bent. Sunlight is a mixture of colour – what we call a spectrum of colours. The raindrops bend some colours more than others, so they are separated out to make the colours of the rainbow.

Sunlight has to pass through the raindrops at a low angle for the colours to show as a semicircular bow. This is why you see rainbows most often after showers in the early morning or late evening, and not at midday. From an aircraft or a mountain top you can sometimes see a rainbow below you as a complete circle.

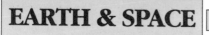

Top-soil (rich in humus)

Sub-soil

Weathered rock

WHAT KIND OF SOIL IS FERTILE?

A fertile soil is rich in humus, bacteria and minerals. It also has enough water and a good texture.

The rock beneath the soil is important. Permeable rocks, such as sandstone, make the soil light and dry. Impermeable rocks, like clay, cause waterlogged soils which hold little air.

Very limey (alkaline) soils are bad for some plants. Broken-down rock fragments provide the minerals which plants need. Climate and natural vegetation are also important. Plants need organic matter, called humus. This contains nutrients plants need for growth.

QUIZ 13

1 What are asteroids?

2 Where might asteroids mostly be found?

3 Which is the largest asteroid?

4 How big is the largest asteroid?

5 How big is the average asteroid?

6 How long is the period of Halley's comet?

7 When was Halley's comet last seen?

8 Of what does a comet's 'tail' consist?

9 When was Comet West first seen?

10 Which comet has the shortest period?

WHY IS A SNOWFLAKE MADE UP OF CRYSTALS?

When water vapour cools, it usually condenses into water droplets. In very cold air the water vapour condenses directly into ice crystals, and these crystals may cling together to make a snowflake.

The temperature of the cloud must be cold enough for ice crystals to form straight from water vapour. The shape of snow crystals varies according to the temperature and humidity of both the air in which they form and the air through which they fall. So it is not surprising that no two crystals are alike. 'Dry' snow falls in cold, dry conditions. It has small crystals and blows into snowdrifts easily. 'Wet' snow forms when the air is moist and warm enough for the crystals to bond together.

WHY DO SAND DUNES MOVE ACROSS DESERTS?

Only about one-fifth of hot deserts are covered with sand. Strong winds often blow in deserts. Because deserts are dry and do not have any vegetation, loose sand can be driven along by the wind. The constant movement of sand from one side of a dune to the other moves the dune.

Deserts are probably getting bigger because there is less rain. Also, strong winds move sand further out to cover the neighbouring land. Bad farming has also led to the soil being worn away, creating deserts.

WHERE IS THE GREAT RIFT VALLEY?

This is a series of linked rift valleys which stretch for 6500 kilometres from north of the River Jordan, via the Dead Sea and the Red Sea, through Ethiopia and East Africa to the coast near the mouth of the Zambezi River.

The Great Rift Valley is between 30 and 60 kilometres wide and has steep scarps on each side for most of its length. The Red Sea fills part of its length. Elsewhere there are long, narrow deep lakes such as Turkana, Mobutu, Tanganyika and Malawi. In East Africa the route of the Rift Valley splits into two branches.

Egypt — Red Sea — Sudan — Ethiopia — Mobutu — L Turkana — L Victoria — L Tanganyika — L Malawi

QUIZ 14

1 What is the core of a comet made of?
2 How big is the core of Halley's comet?
3 When a comet gets near the Sun, what happens?
4 How long is the tail of a comet approaching the Sun?
5 What is a meteor?
6 How big is a meteor when it starts off?
7 What is a meteorite?
8 What is the name of the spectacular meteor shower seen every year on the 12–13 August?
9 Where is the largest meteor crater on Earth?

■ WHERE IS THE EARTH'S CRUST BEING FORMED?

New material is added to the Earth's crust by volcanoes. Much of the lava is molten material from the part of the Earth called the mantle, which lies beneath the solid crust. Some volcanoes are found on land, but many are located deep beneath the oceans where lava flows onto the seabed.

Most scientists believe that the area of the Earth's surface remains the same. So while material is being added to the crust at the junction of some plates, it is being lost at the junctions of others.

■ WHERE IS THE SAN ANDREAS FAULT?

The San Andreas fault is in western California, near the Pacific coast of the USA.

The San Andreas fault and the Fairweather fault in Alaska form the boundary between the Pacific Plate and the North American Plate. The Pacific Plate is slowly rotating anti-clockwise. West of the San Andreas fault, the land is moving north-westwards. As a result, land along the fault is moving at five centimetres every year. Sometimes, however, the movement is more dramatic, leading to earthquakes.

WHERE ARE DIAMONDS AND GOLD FOUND?

Diamonds were formed deep underground in conditions of intense heat and pressure. Artificial diamonds can be made in factories. Pure carbon is baked under great pressure to over 1400 ˚C. Natural diamonds probably formed under similar conditions.

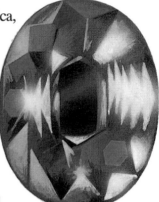

Diamonds are mined in South Africa, Tanzania, Siberia, Africa, India, Indonesia, Brazil, Australia and the former Soviet republics. Gold is found in mineral veins in rocks, or in gravels which have been washed away from areas where gold-bearing rocks have been eroded. Prospectors may pan the gravel in streams for grains of gold. Half of the world's gold is mined in South Africa.

QUIZ 16

1 Why is the setting sun red?

2 What is the Sun's surface gravity?

3 Which element makes up 90% of the Sun?

4 What is the temperature at the centre of the Sun?

5 What happens to hydrogen atoms in the Sun?

6 How many hydrogen atoms are needed to make one atom of helium?

7 How long will the Sun's hydrogen last?

8 What type of star is a Blue Giant?

9 Which will be brighter – our Sun, or a Blue Giant?

WHERE CAN YOU SEE OVER 1500 MILLION YEARS OF ROCK STRATA?

The Colorado Desert in the south-west of the USA has layers of rock which have formed over a period of about 1600 million years. The river Colorado and its tributaries have sliced these layers in the Grand Canyon and other nearby canyons.

The Grand Canyon area is the only place on Earth where geologists can study so many layers of undisturbed rock and an almost perfect sequence of fossils. The 'Granite Gorge' at the bottom of the Grand Canyon is cut into the rocks that form the base of most of North America.

EARTH & SPACE

WHERE IS THE WORLD'S GREATEST MOUNTAIN RANGE?

The greatest mountain range on land is the Himalaya-Karakoram Range to the north of India. It has the most of the world's highest peaks.

In the Himalayas, on the border of Nepal and Tibet, is Mount Everest, the highest mountain on land: 8848 metres high. The height of Mount Everest was discovered in 1852. It was named after Sir George Everest, the Surveyor-General of India at the time. The Andes of South America are a longer but lower mountain range.

WHERE IS THE LARGEST ACTIVE VOLCANO?

The highest active volcanoes on land are in the Andes, in South America. The highest of these is Ojos del Salada, which is 6885 metres high. But even larger volcanoes rise from the floor of the Pacific Ocean and form the islands of Hawaii.

Mauna Loa, on Hawaii, is probably the largest active volcano in the world. It rises 4170 metres above sea level, but its base is 5180 metres below sea level. This base is roughly oval in shape: 119 kilometres long and 85 kilometres across.

The lava from Hawaiian volcanoes is very liquid and flows for long distances. Mauna Loa erupts about every 3.5 years. The nearby Kilauea Crater, south-east of the main volcano, is filled with red-hot lava.

QUIZ 17

1 How many stars are there in our Galaxy?
2 Are they as hot as the Sun?
3 Why is the Sun a special star to us?
4 Is the Sun an unusual sort of star?
5 Are there other Suns with planets?
6 What kind of stars are most common in our Galaxy?
7 What is often called 'the Sun's atmosphere'?
8 When did an eclipse of the Sun halt a battle?
9 When can we see the corona of the Sun?
10 What name do we give to the bright surface of the Sun?

WHICH VOLCANO DESTROYED AN ANCIENT ROMAN TOWN?

Mount Vesuvius rises above the Bay of Naples in southern Italy. In AD 79 this volcano erupted and buried nearby Pompeii. The volcano had been dormant for 800 years. Few people realized it was a volcano.

On 24 August, AD 79, Mount Vesuvius suddenly erupted. For three days, Pompeii was bombarded with pumice and ash. About 16,000 people died.

WHERE IS THE PACIFIC 'RING OF FIRE'?

Seen on a map, the Pacific Ocean appears surrounded by a ring of fiery volcanic activity.

There are many active volcanoes, and some of the world's highest are in the Andes and the mountains of Central America. Others are found in the mountains of the western USA and Alaska, in the Kamchatka peninsula and in Siberia, Japan, Papua New Guinea and New Zealand.

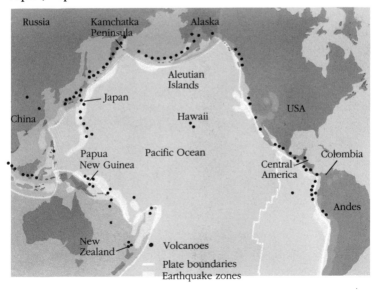

Russia
Kamchatka Peninsula
Alaska
Aleutian Islands
Japan
China
Hawaii
USA
Papua New Guinea
Pacific Ocean
Central America
Colombia
Andes
New Zealand
• Volcanoes
– Plate boundaries
Earthquake zones

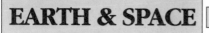

EARTH & SPACE

◼ WHICH ARE THE WORLD'S BIGGEST EXPANSES OF ICE?

Just over 10 per cent of the land surface of the world is permanently covered by ice. Most of the world's ice (87 per cent) is in Antarctica. The Arctic has 12.5 per cent (mainly covering Greenland), and the rest is found in the glaciers which exist on every continent.

The longest glacier is the Lambert-Fisher Ice Passage in Antarctica, which is 515 kilometres long. Petermanns Glacier in Greenland is the largest glacier in the northern hemisphere, 40 kilometres out to sea.

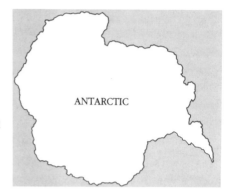

ANTARCTIC

QUIZ 19

1 Who launched the first true rocket vehicle in 1926?

2 How was the first rocket fuelled?

3 What did the Soviet spacecraft Luna 2 achieve?

4 What happened on 13 September 1959?

5 Which spacecraft first reached Venus?

6 Which American craft was first to reach another world?

7 Which craft made the first successful 'soft' landing?

8 What did the spacecraft Surveyor 1 achieve?

◼ WHERE ARE THE BIGGEST ICEBERGS FOUND?

The icebergs with the biggest area are the tabular icebergs that break away from Antarctica. The largest iceberg ever seen was over 31,000 square

kilometres (bigger than Belgium).

The tallest icebergs break away from Greenland. The tallest one ever seen was 167 metres above the water. Eight-ninths of the iceberg was below the sea.

WHERE IS THE LONGEST REEF IN THE WORLD?

The Great Barrier Reef, off the north-east coast of Australia, is the world's longest coral reef. It stretches for over 2000 kilometres from near Papua to the centre of the Queensland coast.

The Great Barrier Reef lies between 45 and 65 kilometres off the Australian coast. In the north it is only 15-20 kilometres wide, but in the south the reef area extends up to 325 kilometres out to sea.

WHERE ARE FIORDS FOUND?

Fiords are long, narrow steep-sided inlets of the sea. They were made by glaciers which deepened the valleys along which they flowed. After the glaciers disappeared, their U-shaped valleys were flooded by the sea to form fiords.

Fiords are found on mountainous coasts which have been eroded by glaciers. The fiords of Norway are famous and are among the longest in the world. Sogne Fiord is 183 kilometres long, and its average width is 4.75 kilometres. It is 1245 metres deep. Fiords are also found along the coasts of Iceland, Greenland and New Zealand.

WHERE ARE THE WORLD'S HOTTEST PLACES?

The highest shade temperature on record is 58 °C in September 1922 at Al'Aziziyah in the Sahara Desert in Libya. Nearly as hot was the 56.7 °C recorded in Death Valley in the USA in July 1913.

The eastern Sahara has more sunshine than anywhere else: sunshine has been recorded for 4300 hours in a year, which is an average of 11 hours 47 minutes per day.

QUIZ 21

1 How old are the oldest of the Earth's rocks found so far?
2 How old is the Earth?
3 What is the total surface area of the Earth?
4 How do scientists know the Earth's age?
5 When did the Earth's crust first become solid?
6 Was there ever ice in the Sahara?
7 What was Pangaea?
8 When did Pangaea exist?
9 Where was the Sahara originally situated?
10 Where did the Equator once run?

WHERE ARE THE WORLD'S COLDEST PLACES?

The coldest temperatures are recorded in winter in Antarctica. In July 1983, Russian scientists measured a new record low of -89.2 °C.

Very cold temperatures have been recorded in Siberia: -68°C at Verkhoyansk in 1892. This place holds the record for the greatest temperature range: from a coldest winter temperature of -68°C to a hottest summer temperature of 36.7°C. The Arctic 'cold pole' is some way from the North Pole because of the surrounding Arctic Ocean. Seas have a moderating effect on the climate of coastal areas.

WHERE ARE THE WETTEST PLACES ON EARTH?

Cherrapunji, in India, holds the record for the most rain in one month: 9299 millimetres in July 1861. It also had the most rain in a year: 26,461 millimetres in the year up to 31 July 1861.

Mount Wai-'ale-'ale in Hawaii has the most rainy days (350 a year), and the highest average annual rainfall. Its annual rainfall is 11,680 millimetres. The three wettest counties are Sierra Leone, Malaysia and Colombia.

QUIZ 22

1 What are the continents of the Old World?

2 What are the continents of the New World?

3 When did the Atlantic open up?

4 What is the name of the ocean 250 million years ago?

5 Was America ever joined to Asia?

6 Why are the Alps higher than the Caledonian mountains in Scotland?

7 How long ago were the Alps formed?

8 How did the Alps form?

WHERE IS THE DRIEST PLACE ON EARTH?

In the Atacama Desert in northern Chile, the first rain for 400 years fell in 1971. All deserts are dry, but the Atacama is the driest.

Cairo, in the eastern Sahara, averages 28 millimetres of rain a year, and Bahrain on the edge of the Arabian Desert, has 81 millimetres. Not all the dry parts of the Earth are also hot – the Polar lands are also very dry.

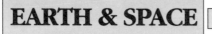

WHAT IS AN ATOLL?

An atoll is a coral reef which forms an almost complete circle around a lagoon.

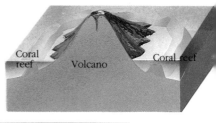

The circular coral reefs of most atolls reach deep down into water where no coral can grow. As the diagram shows, atolls may once have been reefs in shallow water surrounding a volcano. As the island sinks, or the sea-level changes, the coral continues to grow. The original island disappears far below the lagoon, and the reef forms an atoll.

QUIZ 23

1 What was the Mediterranean like 6 million years ago?

2 What have boreholes revealed beneath the present Mediterranean sea?

3 What was the climate like there 6 million years ago?

4 Were there many rivers?

5 What shape did the ancient Greeks believe the Earth to be?

6 How did Pythagoras describe the shape of the Earth?

7 How did the Greeks know the shape of the Earth?

8 What did the Greeks consider to be the perfect shape?

WHERE ARE THE DOLDRUMS?

The Doldrums is a name given by early sailors to a zone at the Equator where winds are often light, their direction uncertain and where sailing ships were often becalmed.

The exact location of the Doldrums moves with the seasons. In June they are about 5° north of the Equator, and in December they are about 5° south.

WHAT DOES THE SEA BED LOOK LIKE?

The sea bed has cliffs, plateaus, canyons, volcanoes, mountain ranges and deep trenches.

The continental shelf slopes gently away from the beaches surrounding dry land. At a depth of about 180 metres it ends at the steep continental slope.

This huge cliff around the continents is gashed with deep gorges. The deep ocean floor, with its volcanoes and deep trenches, begins at the bottom of the continental slope.

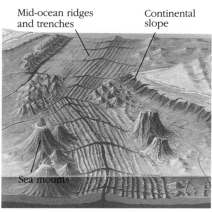

Mid-ocean ridges and trenches

Continental slope

Sea mounts

WHERE IS THE GREATEST OCEAN CURRENT?

The greatest ocean current is in the West Wind Drift (also called the Antarctic Circumpolar Current). Its cold waters originate near the Antarctic and encircle that continent. The current is driven by strong westerly winds.

The West Wind Drift varies in width from 200 to 300 kilometres. Its surface flow is less than one kilometre an hour. Measurements made in Drake Passage, where the current is squeezed between South America and Antarctica, recorded a flow of water at 270 million cubic metres per second. The Gulf Stream is a warm ocean current which begins in the Gulf of Mexico and flows across the North Atlantic towards Europe. It is a meandering current about 100 kilometres wide, and its average speed is less than one kilometre an hour.

QUIZ 24

1 When does the earliest recorded sea-chart date from?
2 Who used the earliest sea-chart?
3 How did early navigators operate?
4 Where does the oldest known map date from?
5 **When** does the oldest known map date from?
6 What did the earliest known map show?
7 What ancient peoples used maps?
8 To what use were the earliest maps put?
9 Who started scientific map-making?

WHERE IS THE DEEPEST PART OF THE OCEAN?

The deepest part of the ocean was found in 1951 by the survey ship **Challenger**. *Echo-soundings showed part of the Mariana Trench, south of Japan, to be 10,900 metres deep.*

In 1960 the US Navy bathyscaphe *Trieste* descended to the bottom of the Challenger Deep. The Mariana Trench is one of many deep trenches around the edges of the Pacific Ocean. These V-shaped trenches are parallel to a continent or line of islands.

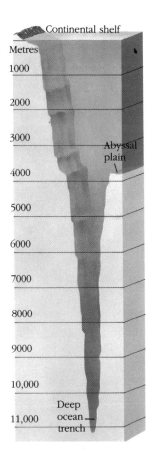

Continental shelf
Metres
1000
2000
3000
Abyssal plain
4000
5000
6000
7000
8000
9000
10,000
11,000 Deep ocean trench

QUIZ 25

1 Who made the first atlas?
2 How were maps first produced?
3 When was the earliest printed map?
4 Who produced the first modern type of atlas?
5 Why is an atlas so called?
6 Who took the first aerial photographs?
7 From what point were the photographs taken?
8 Where and when were they taken?
9 Why were the aerial photographs taken?
10 When did aerial photography really come into use?

WHICH SEA IS THE SALTIEST?

The Dead Sea, on the borders of Israel and Jordan, is the world's saltiest sea – over ten times saltier than the average ocean.

The Dead Sea has no exit. Most of the water comes from the north, in the River Jordan. Mineral springs at the bottom of the Dead Sea and around its shores add to the salts in the water. The climate is very hot and dry, so an enormous amount of water is lost by evaporation. Salts in the water are therefore very concentrated. They are extracted in large evaporation pans.

The shores of the Dead Sea are the lowest exposed point on the Earth's surface – 393 metres below sea level. It has an area of 1020 square kilometres.

IN WHAT WAYS DO RIVERS CHANGE THE SHAPE OF THE LAND?

Rivers can erode land and deposit eroded material further down-stream.

In the upper part of its course, the river flows down steep slopes. Rocks are bounced along by the water and help to erode the river bed. A V-shaped valley is formed. On lower land, the river meanders. River currents undercut the outside of the meanders and deposit sand and mud on the inside of the meanders. This widens the valley. At times of flood the river can damage to low lying land, and its course may be straightened. Old meanders are cut off to form oxbow lakes.

WHERE DOES YOUR TAP WATER COME FROM?

We break into the water cycle to obtain our water. Then we purify it and pipe it to our homes.

Rainwater can be collected from the roof and stored in tanks. In some places water is pumped out of rivers or lakes and piped to homes. Elsewhere, the water we use comes from underground springs or boreholes. It is pumped up from permeable rocks such as chalk. But in most large cities, there is not enough surface water or underground water for everyone, and water may be stored nearby, in huge reservoirs.

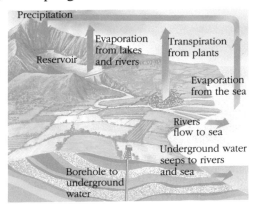

Precipitation

Reservoir

Evaporation from lakes and rivers

Transpiration from plants

Evaporation from the sea

Rivers flow to sea

Underground water seeps to rivers and sea

Borehole to underground water

EARTH & SPACE

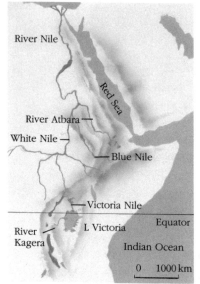

WHICH IS THE LONGEST RIVER?

The three longest rivers in the world are the Nile in Africa: 6670 kilometres long; the Amazon in South America: 6448 kilometres long; and the Mississippi-Missouri in North America: 5970

The river Amazon is larger than the river Nile and contains far more water. Boats can travel much further upstream. The average discharge of the Nile is 3120 cubic metres per second, and the Amazon has an average discharge of 180,000 cubic metres per second.

QUIZ 27

1 When did dinosaurs become extinct?

2 How long had dinosaurs been on Earth?

3 Does anyone know why they died out?

4 Did any other animals die out, too?

5 How big was Tyrannosaurus?

6 Is it true all dinosaurs had small brains?

7 Why do geologists study fossils?

8 Which kind of fossils are most useful to geologists?

WHERE ARE THE HIGHEST WATERFALLS?

The highest falls in the world are the Angel Falls on the Carrao River, a tributary of the Caroni River, in Venezuela, South America. The total fall of water is 979 metres; the longest single drop is 807 metres.

The second highest falls are the Tugela Falls in Natal, South Africa, on the Tugela River, which drops 947 metres at the Falls. The Angel Falls are located on the Auyán-Tepui Mountain. They have long been known to the local Indians who call them Cherun-Meru. Europeans first saw them in 1910. They were re-discovered in 1937 by an American pilot named Jimmy Angel who crash-landed nearby.

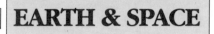

QUIZ 28

1 Where was the oldest coal mine in Britain founded?

2 Are there plants in the Antarctic?

3 How did plants live in the Antarctic?

4 Is there any coal in the Antarctic?

5 What is the crust of the Earth?

6 How do the plates in the crust move?

7 How much oil was spilt when the Exxon Valdez struck a reef?

8 What kind of seas fill up with sediments?

WHERE IS THE LARGEST LAKE?

The world's largest lake is the Caspian Sea, between Iran and the Russian Commonwealth. Although it is

called a sea, it is not connected with the oceans, but is a very large inland lake. Its total area is 371,800 square kilometres. It is in a desert, so a lot of water evaporates, and the water is very salty.

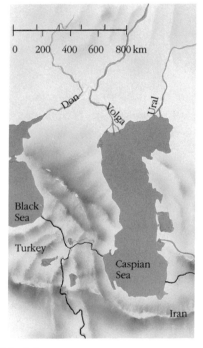

The largest fresh water lake is Lake Superior, between the USA and Canada. It covers 82,350 square kilometres. The world's highest lake is an unnamed glacial lake near Mount Everest. It is 5880 metres above sea level. Lake Titicaca is the highest navigable lake.

WHERE IS THE BIGGEST CAVE?

The largest single cave in the world is the Sarawak Chamber in Sarawak, Eastern Malaysia.

The largest cave system in the world is under the Mammoth Cave National Park in the US state of Kentucky. The deepest cave discovered so far is the Gouffre Jean Bernard Cave in the French Alps. In 1982, a team of French cavers reached 1494 metres below the surface.

WHERE ARE STALACTITES AND STALAGMITES?

These features are found in limestone caves. They are formed from a rock which is sometimes called 'dripstone'. Stalactites are columns of dripstone hanging down from the ceiling, and stalagmites rise from the floor.

Limestone is mainly made of calcium carbonate. When rainwater seeps through cracks in this rock it reacts with the calcium carbonate and other minerals. Each drip hangs for a while, and tiny deposits of calcium carbonate are left. Very slowly, these deposits grow to form stalactites. Drips reaching the floor of the cave gradually become stalagmites.

WHAT WOULD HAPPEN IF ALL THE WORLD'S ICE MELTED?

If all the ice in the world melted, new land would be revealed in the Arctic and the Antarctic and in some mountains. But large areas of the world would be flooded as sea-level rose.

Sea-level has changed in the past during glacials and inter-glacials, so it may change in the future. If the world's ice melted, sea-level would rise by at least 65 metres. Denmark would be flooded, and many great capitals such as London, Dublin, Paris, Rome and Helsinki would be drowned.

QUIZ 29

1 What is the lava thrown out by a volcano made of?

2 Where does molten rock come from?

3 What is this molten rock called?

4 Where would you find the Earth's mantle?

5 When was the longest lava flow in history

6 What does magma contain?

7 Where do earthquakes occur?

8 How many earthquakes cause damage every year?

WHERE IS THERE SNOW NEAR THE EQUATOR?

Snow lies on the ground all year in places where the temperature is low enough to prevent it melting completely. Although it is hot at sea level at the Equator, it can get very cold at the top of high mountains.

Some Equatorial mountains are high enough to have permanent snow, such as Mount Kilimanjaro in East Africa and the peaks of the Andes in Ecuador. Mount Kilimanjaro rises high above the East African plains on the borders of Kenya and Tanzania. The highest point is 5894 metres above sea level.

QUIZ 30

1 Where in the world do geysers occur?
2 Do all volcanic areas have geysers?
3 What causes a geyser to spout?
4 Which kitchen utensil could be said to operate like a geyser?
5 What happens to the air when you climb a mountain?
6 How far away is the Sun?
7 Does the Sun heat the Earth, or the air?
8 How does the Sun's energy reach us?
9 Which is the tallest geyser in the world?
10 Where would you find 'Old Faithful?'

WHERE IS MONUMENT VALLEY?

Monument Valley is part of the Colorado Plateau, in the dry south-west of the USA.

The towers, columns and castle-like masses of rock shown in the photograph are completely natural monuments. They are mainly sandstones and other sedimentary rocks.

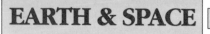
WHAT ARE OIL AND NATURAL GAS?

Oil and natural gas are fossil fuels. They formed from the remains of tiny plants and animals which

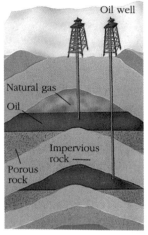

once lived in tropical seas. They were changed by chemical processes into gases and liquids.

Oil and gas collect in porous rocks, which allow liquids to soak through. They are trapped between impervious rocks, which will not allow liquids to pass through. Some oil wells pump oil from a huge area, but others tap only a small area and soon run dry.

QUIZ 31

1 Where does the salt in the sea come from?

2 How much ordinary salt is there in the sea?

3 Where is the sea most salty?

4 Which is the saltiest place in the world?

5 Which is one of the least salty seas?

6 What is sodium chloride?

7 What causes tides?

8 How often do high tides take place?

9 Do they vary very much in time?

10 How long does it take the Moon to travel round the Earth?

WHAT IS COAL?

Coal is a rock which is burned as fuel. It is called a 'fossil fuel' because it formed from the remains of trees and plants millions of years ago. Imprints of these plants can be found on some lumps of coal.

Coal is usually found in layers, called seams, of different thicknesses sandwiched between other rocks which formed at the same time. The oldest known coal seams are about 360 million years old.

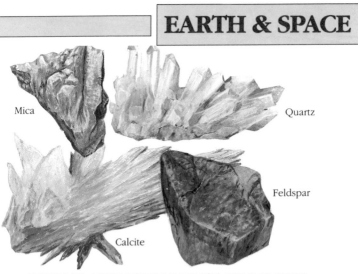

Mica

Quartz

Feldspar

Calcite

WHAT ARE THE MOST COMMON ROCK-FORMING MINERALS?

The majority of minerals found in the rocks of the Earth's crust are silicates.

The Earth's crust is made up of different kinds of rocks. Most sedimentary rocks formed from accumulations of minerals which were weathered out of igneous rocks. Most of these minerals will be silicates. Silicates are a large group of minerals, all of which contain silica and oxygen. The commonest silicate family is feldspar.

WHY ARE ROCKS USED FOR BUILDING?

Rocks are used as building materials because they resist weathering. Usually such rocks are hard and often they are beautiful too. Rocks that are easily quarried and shaped for building are especially important. Granite is an example. Softer rocks such as clay and sand are dug up and made into harder building materials such as bricks and concrete.

Many old buildings are built of local stone or bricks. When transport was difficult, only the richest people could afford to import special stone.

QUIZ 32

1 What kind of cloud is thin and almost transparent?
2 Is there always water vapour in the air?
3 Can some air hold more water vapour?
4 What happens when air cools down?
5 What type of cloud looks 'puffy'?
6 When tiny water droplets form bigger drops, what happens?
7 What is fog?
8 What is lightning?
9 Where is the most thundery region on Earth?

QUIZ 33

1 Which objects get struck most by lightning?

2 Why should trees get struck?

3 How does a lightning flash begin?

4 How can tall buildings be protected against lightning?

5 What are lightning conductors made of?

6 How fast does lightning travel on the downward stroke?

7 What is a hailstone?

8 What does a hailstone look like inside?

9 Where are hailstones likely to fall?

10 How heavy was the heaviest hailstone ever?

WHAT IS ARTESIAN WATER?

Artesian water is underground water which rises to the surface under natural pressure. The name comes from Artois in France, where many wells have been dug to reach artesian water in the underlying chalk.

Rain falling on higher land can flow through the layers of porous rocks. Beneath the low land, the porous rocks are sandwiched between impervious layers. The water-bearing layer is called an aquifer. The Great Artesian Basin of Australia is the world's largest.

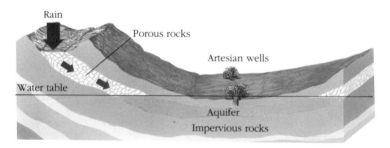

WHERE HAS LAND RECLAMATION DOUBLED THE SIZE OF A COUNTRY?

The Netherlands is one of the smallest countries in Europe. Yet half its land area is the result of reclaiming land from beneath marshes, lakes and the sea.

The areas of reclaimed land are called polders. They are surrounded by dykes (banks) to keep out flood-water, and criss-crossed by drainage ditches. The water was once removed by wind pumps, but diesel pumps are used now. Major reclamation projects include the Zuider Zee and Delta Projects. The Zuider Zee was transformed into the freshwater Lake IJssel by a 32-kilometre-long dam. Five huge polders totalling 2260 square kilometres were created.

Colorado sand dunes

WHERE ARE DESERTS BEING CREATED?

On the edges of some of the Earth's natural deserts, the environment is being upset by poor farming methods and mismanagement.

Semi-desert areas have fragile soils and difficult climates. Several good years are often followed by several bad years. In the good years, farmers may extend the cultivated areas, or increase their flocks and herds and dig more wells. But in a series of dry years, crops fail, animals exhaust the pasture, the bare soil is eroded and many wells dry up. Such problems created the 'dust bowl' in the USA in the 1930s and extended the Sahara in the 1970s.

QUIZ 34

1 What is a snowflake formed from?
2 Can any two snowflakes be the same?
3 How are ice crystals formed?
4 What are typhoons and cyclones?
5 What is a hurricane?
6 How fast does the fastest hurricane travel?
7 How far across is the biggest hurricane?
8 What happens to sunlight when it passes through raindrops?
9 What do the raindrops do to the colours in sunlight?
10 How many different colours can we see in a rainbow?

WHERE IS THE REMOTEST PLACE ON EARTH?

Only one-fifth of the Earth is densely populated, so there are still plenty of remote places. The remotest inhabited land is Tristan da Cunha, a volcanic island in the South Atlantic.

This tiny island covers just 98 square kilometres. Its nearest neighbour is the island of St Helena, 2120 kilometres to the north-east. In 1961 Tristan da Cunha erupted and all its inhabitants were evacuated. They returned in 1963.

EARTH & SPACE

WHICH IS THE MOST SPARSELY POPULATED CONTINENT?

Antarctica has no permanent settlement, but the most sparsely populated country is Greenland.

The remotest island is Bouvet Island, an uninhabited Norwegian dependency in the South Atlantic. The nearest land is 1700 kilometres away, and that is the uninhabited coast of Antarctica.

QUIZ 35

1 What do we call a silted up area at the mouth of the river?

2 Why is it so called?

3 How is a delta formed?

4 Where is the largest delta in the world?

5 Name a European river which has a delta.

6 Do many lakes disappear altogether?

7 What happens when a lake disappears?

8 Where is Lake Eyre?

9 What can cause a lake to disappear?

10 Where is Lake Superior?

WHERE IS RICE GROWN?

Rice provides more food for more people than any other cereal crop in the world. It is the basic food crop in much of southern and eastern Asia.

Rice needs hot weather and plenty of water. The water may come from heavy rain, such as the monsoon rains of Asia, or from irrigation. Rice needs flat land, because the water level in the fields must be carefully controlled. Many hillsides in Asia are terraced to get enough flat land.

WHERE IS TEA GROWN?

The tea we drink is made from the crushed leaves of an evergreen bush which grows in hot, damp climates. It seems to thrive at quite high altitudes, up to 2300 metres, in tropical areas.

Tea was brought to Europe from China. As the drink became fashionable, plantations of tea bushes were planted by the Dutch in Indonesia and by the British in India and Sri Lanka. Now tea plantations are also found in Japan, East Africa and on hillsides in Georgia in Asia.

WHERE DOES COTTON COME FROM?

The cotton thread we sew with or weave into cloth is spun from fibres in the cotton boll. This is the seed pod of the cotton plant.

Cotton was a major crop in south-eastern USA, which still produces nearly a fifth of the world's cotton. Egypt and Sudan also export cotton. It is important, too, in parts of East Africa, India and Pakistan, China and South America.

QUIZ 36

1 How can one describe a glacier?
2 Where do glaciers appear?
3 Where on Earth is the greatest thickness of ice?
4 Do glaciers move?
5 When do most glaciers date from?
6 How many glaciation periods have there been?
7 What does a soil need to be fertile?
8 Is sandstone a permeable or impermeable rock?
9 What kind of a rock is clay?
10 What do rock fragments do to the soil?

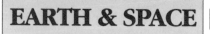

WHERE IS THE WORLD'S LARGEST ARTIFICIAL LAKE?

The artificial lake with the greatest area is Lake Volta in Ghana, West Africa. The Bratsk Reservoir on the Angara River, south-east Siberia, in Russia, holds the greatest volume of water in an artificial lake.

The Akosombo Dam was completed across the River Volta in 1965. The dam is built at the southern end of a gorge, and produces hydro-electric power.

Lake Volta began to build up behind the damn in the valley of the river Volta. Altogether the lake now covers 8842 square kilometres and has a shoreline 7250 kilometres long.

QUIZ 37

1 How much of the hot desert is covered by sand?
2 What are the winds like in the desert?
3 What happens when strong winds blow?
4 Why are some deserts getting bigger?
5 What happens to neighbouring land?
6 Does the Earth's crust go on forming?
7 Where does the new material come from?
8 Is the Earth's crust being destroyed?
9 Does the area of the Earth remain the same?

WHERE DOES RUBBER COME FROM?

Natural rubber is made from latex, a milky fluid which is found under the bark of the rubber tree. This tree is a native of the Amazon rain forest and grows in hot, wet equatorial conditions.

The rubber tree was introduced to South-East Asia via London's botanical gardens at Kew. Plantations in Malaysia and Indonesia have supplied much of the world's rubber. The bark of the rubber tree is cut and the latex oozes into a cup fixed by the rubber tapper. The latex is then smoked and vulcanized to make rubber.

WHERE WAS MAIZE FIRST GROWN?

Maize is grown in many parts of the world which have hot summers. It is a native of the Americas, and was an important food crop for many Indians before the Europeans arrived.

For the early European settlers in America, 'Indian corn' as it was called, was often a life saver. Most American maize is now used as cattle food, but some is eaten as sweetcorn or turned into cornflakes or flour.

QUIZ 38

1 Where is the San Andreas fault?

2 Is California on the Pacific or Atlantic coast of the USA?

3 In what direction is the land moving, west of the Andreas fault?

4 In what direction does the Pacific Plate rotate?

5 In what continent is the Great Rift Valley?

6 How long is the Great Rift Valley?

7 How wide is the Great Rift Valley?

8 Which is the world's oldest known rock?

9 How old is it?

WHERE DOES COCOA COME FROM?

Cocoa is made from the beans which develop in the large pod of the cacao tree. Cocoa was drunk by the Aztecs of Central America before Europeans arrived.

The cacao tree is still grown in areas of Central and South America, but most cocoa now comes from West Africa. The tropical cacao tree grows near the Equator.

WHEN WAS THE FIRST ATLAS PRODUCED?

The first collection of maps to be called an atlas was published by Gerardus Mercator in 1585. Until printing was invented, maps were very expensive.

In 1477, a Latin version of Ptolemy's Geographia was printed. Abraham Ortelius produced the first modern type of atlas in 1570. At the same time, Gerardus Mercator was working on a series of volumes, which he called 'Atlas' after the Greek god who symbolized the study of heaven and earth.

QUIZ 39

1 Where can millions of years of rock strata be studied?

2 How old are the rocks?

3 Where may diamonds be found?

4 Can diamonds be made artificially?

5 What temperature is needed to make diamonds?

6 How long ago were diamonds formed?

7 Where is gold found?

8 Where were the famous gold rushes?

9 Why do prospectors pan the gravel in streams?

10 Where was a rich gold find made in 1980?

WHEN WAS AERIAL PHOTOGRAPHY FIRST USED FOR MAP-MAKING?

The first aerial photographs were taken from a balloon above Paris in 1858.

The photographer and balloonist was Gaspard Felix Tournachon, who was also known as Nadar. These first air photographs of Paris were used to help with mapmaking. Experiments continued with balloons and kites, but it was after World War I that aerial photography became useful.

WHAT IS CROP ROTATION?

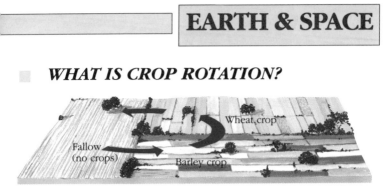

Some crops are able to put goodness back into the soil. Farmers can improve soil by growing different kinds of crops after each other in the same fields. This is known as crop rotation.

Variations on the medieval three-field system have been used in Europe for over 2000 years. In the three-field system, fields are divided into strips which are cultivated by different farmers.

WHEN WAS SUGAR INTRODUCED TO EUROPE?

Sugar-making may have started in India about 3000 BC. Alexander the Great took samples home to Greece. By the 8th century, Arabs were making sugar in Spain and France.

Christopher Columbus took sugar cane from Europe to the West Indies in 1493, and for many years sugar was an expensive luxury. In Tudor times it was used as a medicine. Gradually sugar plantations were established in many parts of the New World. The sugar trade across the Atlantic became very important.

Sugar beet

Sugar cane

QUIZ 40

1 What is the Himalaya-Karakoram Range?
2 Which is the world's highest mountain?
3 How high is it?
4 Who was it named after?
5 Which is a longer range of mountains?
6 Which mountain range has the most active volcanoes?
7 Which is the highest of these mountains?
8 Which is the largest active volcano in the world?
9 How high is it above sea level?
10 How often does Mauna Loa erupt?

EARTH & SPACE

WHEN WAS THE SAHARA COVERED WITH ICE?

Geologists have found evidence of glaciation in the bedrock of the Algerian desert. This suggests that the Sahara was covered by ice about 450 million years ago. Further studies suggest that when this happened the area was near the South Pole.

This is possible because the shape and position of continents on our globe has not always been the same. The continents are made up of 'plates', which move continually, although very slowly, on the molten mantle of the Earth.

QUIZ 41

1 Where is Mount Vesuvius?

2 What happened in AD 79 after 800 years?

3 What happened to Pompeii in that year?

4 How many people died?

5 What did the volcanic ash preserve for the future?

6 With what does the Pacific Ocean appear to be surrounded?

7 How many active volcanoes are there in the world?

8 Are there any volcanoes in North America?

9 What are the Aleutians?

10 Can active volcanoes be found in Asia?

WHEN WAS THE EARTH FORMED?

The oldest rocks found so far are thought to be about 3850 million years old - so the Earth had a solid crust by then. Some meteorites and pieces of Moon rock are probably 4600 years old, so scientists think that the Earth formed about 4600 million years ago.

Scientists measure the Earth's age by studying the rate of decay of radioactive elements with special equipment. This technique is called carbon-dating.

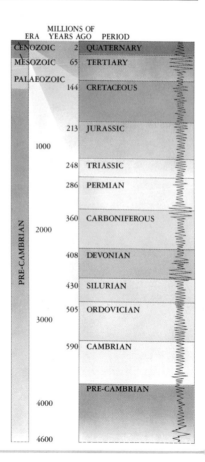

ERA	MILLIONS OF YEARS AGO	PERIOD
CENOZOIC	2	QUATERNARY
MESOZOIC	65	TERTIARY
PALAEOZOIC		
	144	CRETACEOUS
	213	JURASSIC
	1000	
	248	TRIASSIC
	286	PERMIAN
	360	CARBONIFEROUS
	2000	
	408	DEVONIAN
	430	SILURIAN
	505	ORDOVICIAN
	3000	
	590	CAMBRIAN
PRE-CAMBRIAN		PRE-CAMBRIAN
	4000	
	4600	

QUIZ 42

1 Where was the highest shade temperature on record?

2 Where is the hottest place in the USA?

3 What place has more sunshine than anywhere else?

4 How many hours sunshine does the Sahara have in a year?

5 Which is the coldest place in the world?

6 What is the lowest temperature on record?

7 Which place has the greatest temperature range?

8 What is frost?

9 When does it form?

WHY IS THERE LIFE ON THE EARTH?

All life will die if it becomes too hot or too cold, or if there is no air to breathe. No other planet in the Solar System has the right conditions for Earth-like life.

Living cells, but these cells need substances containing elements such as hydrogen, oxygen and nitrogen if they are to survive. The Earth is the only planet with large amounts of water and oxygen. Both are essential for life.

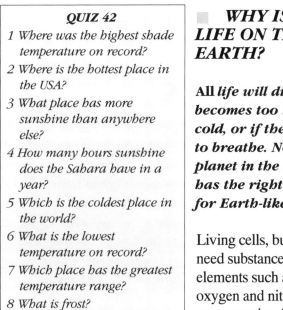

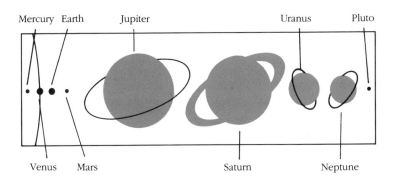

Mercury Earth Jupiter Uranus Pluto

Venus Mars Saturn Neptune

WHY DO THE PLANETS REVOLVE AROUND THE SUN?

If the planets did not move, the Sun's pull would drag them inwards. But if they moved too quickly, they would fly off into space. The closer a planet is to the Sun, the faster it must move.

The planets all move in the same direction. They were probably formed from the same spinning cloud of material that produced the Sun. At birth, the Sun would have been spinning on its axis in a few hours. The cloud's pull slowed it down to its present 25-day period.

Apart from Venus and Uranus, all the planets spin in an anti-clockwise direction too. Venus spins very slowly backwards, while the axis of Uranus is tilted right over, so that it spins on its side.

45

EARTH & SPACE

WHAT IS THE DIFFERENCE BETWEEN A PLANET AND A MOON?

A planet is a dark body orbiting a star. All the planets in the Solar System reflect light from the Sun. A moon (or satellite) also shines by reflection, but it revolves around a planet.

Of the nine planets, only Mercury and Venus have no known satellites. Spacecraft have helped to discover 16 satellites around Jupiter. Saturn has the largest satellite in the Solar System, Titan.

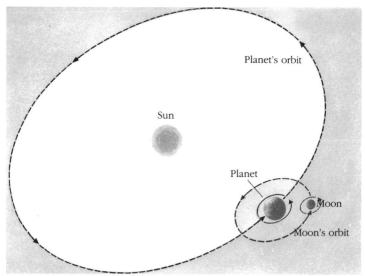

WHY IS THE MOON COVERED WITH CRATERS?

The planets and satellites of the Solar System were formed when much smaller bodies collided together. Long after these worlds had taken shape, their surfaces were cratered by later collisions.

The lunar craters were probably formed during the first few hundred million years of the Moon's 4500-million year history. There is no atmosphere to produce winds and weather, which could have worn these features away.

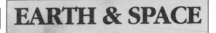
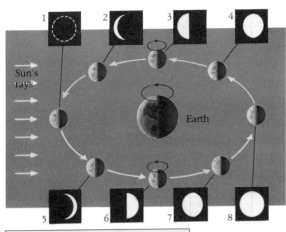

Sun's rays

Earth

1 New Moon
2 Waxing crescent
3 Last quarter
4 Waning gibbous
5 Waning crescent
6 First quarter
7 Waxing gibbous
8 Full Moon

QUIZ 44

1 How much of the world's land is always covered with ice?

2 How much of the world's ice is in Antarctica?

3 How much of the world's ice is in the Arctic?

4 What is permafrost?

5 Where is it found?

6 Permafrost has been found up to 1370 metres deep. Where?

7 How big was the world's largest iceberg?

8 Where do the tallest icebergs come from?

9 How tall was the tallest iceberg ever seen?

10 How tall are the ice cliffs of Antarctica?

WHY DOES THE MOON WAX AND WANE?

The Sun can shine on only one half or hemisphere of the Moon. As it orbits the Earth every month, our view of this half changes.

At New Moon this half of the Moon is turned away from the Earth, and cannot be seen, while at Full it is turned towards us. The time as the Moon 'grows' from New to Full is called 'waxing'. After Full, the Moon 'wanes' or shrinks to invisibility once more.

WHY DOES THE MOON KEEP THE SAME FACE TOWARDS THE EARTH?

When it was first formed, the Moon was probably spinning rapidly. But the Earth's gravitational pull has slowed it down. The Moon now turns on its axis in the same time that it takes to orbit around the Earth. This means that the same face is always pointing inwards, towards the Earth.

Eclipses of the Moon occur when the Earth casts a long shadow into space, away from the Sun. If the Moon passes through this shadow, it grows dim.

WHY IS THE NEW MOON INVISIBLE?

The true New Moon lies almost between the Earth and the Sun. The Sun is so dazzling that nothing can be seen near it. At the same time, the dark hemisphere of the Moon is turned towards the Earth.

The crescent Moon is usually first noticed in the evening sky about two days after New Moon. The best time to look for a very young Moon is just after sunset in the spring, or, for an old Moon, at dawn in the autumn.

QUIZ 45

1 Which is the greatest ocean current?
2 Where does this current originate?
3 How is this current driven along?
4 Which is the largest gulf in the world?
5 Which of all the world's seas has the clearest water?
6 Who named the Doldrums?
7 Where are the Doldrums located in June?
8 What is the Gulf Stream?
9 How wide is the Gulf Stream?
10 Where are the world's strongest currents?

WHY IS THERE NO LIFE ON THE MOON?

The life-forms that are familiar to us need air and water, as well as protection from some dangerous rays sent out by the Sun.

The Moon has no atmosphere, no water on its surface, and is completely exposed to space. Also the temperature at midday is higher than that of boiling water. To find out if any living organisms could survive on the Moon's surface, scientists built special chambers. These copied the Moon's conditions exactly. Even simple bacteria died.

WHY IS MARS RED?

The rocks on the surface of Mars contain iron, which has turned to a kind of rust. This red, dusty material covers the planet's surface and is sometimes blown into huge dust storms.

On Mars, the 'Red Planet', dust is so fine that it hangs in the thin air as a permanent haze, causing the sky to be pink rather than dark blue. Sometimes the surface of Mars disappears from sight beneath clouds of dust raised by Martian winds.

WHICH PLANET SPINS THE FASTEST?

Jupiter, which is the largest of the planets in the Solar System, spins on its axis in the shortest time, only 9 hours and 50 minutes.

The next fastest planet is its giant neighbour Saturn, with a 'day' of 10 hours and 16 minutes. Jupiter is much less solid than the Earth, and this causes different parts of its surface to rotate in different times. When an object spins, an effect known as centrifugal force makes it begin to fly apart. This makes Jupiter's equatorial regions bulge outwards by about 5000 kilometres so it is not a perfect sphere.

QUIZ 46

1 How deep is the deepest part of the Pacific ocean?
2 When was this depth discovered?
3 Is it possible for anyone to reach the bottom of the ocean here?
4 Which sea is the saltiest?
5 Where is it?
6 Why is it so salty?
7 What is an archipelago?
8 Where is the largest archipelago?
9 How many islands make up the country of Indonesia?
10 Which is the largest bay in the world?

WHY IS VENUS SO HOT?

The atmosphere of Venus is about 90 times as thick as our own. Although it is always cloudy, enough sunlight breaks through to heat the rocky ground during its four-year 'day'. The thick atmosphere acts like a blanket and holds heat in.

The midday temperature is 480°C, as hot as an oven turned fully on. Venus could not support life as we know it. The clouds consist of concentrated sulphuric acid!

WHY IS MERCURY DIFFICULT TO SEE?

The innermost planet, Mercury, seems to swing out first on one side and then on the other side of the Sun. These appearances are known as 'elongations'.

At eastern elongation (to the left of the Sun, as seen from the northern hemisphere) Mercury is low in the western sky after sunset. At western elongation it rises in the dawn sky. At these times, it looks like a star. Mercury takes about 116 days to return to the same elongation, so there are three morning and three evening elongations each year. Spring elongations and autumn morning elongations are the easiest to see, but Mercury is never very obvious to observers in northern Europe. It is obscured by the Sun's glare.

QUIZ 47

1 What is the Great Barrier Reef formed from?
2 How long is it?
3 Where is the Great Barrier Reef?
4 Where is the largest atoll in the world?
5 What are fiords?
6 In what shape valley is a fiord formed?
7 Which country is famed for its fiords?
8 How long is Sogne Fiord in Norway?
9 Where else are fiords found?
10 What is the deepest canyon in the world?

WHY DOES SATURN HAVE RINGS?

Nobody knows this for sure. The rings are made up of countless pieces of rock and ice a few centimetres across. They could be the remains of a satellite, or moon, that broke away many millions of years ago.

Saturn's ring system is about 22 times the diameter of the Earth, but it is only a few kilometres thick. The particles are like a blizzard in orbit around the planet's equator.

WHY ARE THE GIANT PLANETS GASEOUS?

The Sun and the planets of the Solar System formed from a huge cloud of gas and tiny solid particles about 4600 million years ago. Small planets like the Earth lost a lot of hydrogen into space, but the giant planets kept all of theirs.

QUIZ 48

1 *Which is the world longest river?*
2 *How long is the Amazon?*
3 *Which is the largest river in the world?*
4 *Which is the longest river in North America?*
5 *What is the average discharge of the Amazon?*
6 *Where are the Angel Falls?*
7 *How high are the Angel Falls?*
8 *Where are the Tugela Falls?*
9 *Which is the muddiest river in the world?*
10 *The Hwang-ho flooded in 1931 – how many people died?*

The pull of gravity of the giant planets is much stronger than that of the Earth. A person standing on Jupiter (supposing it had a solid surface) would feel three times as heavy. This pull of gravity prevents the hydrogen from escaping into space. Hydrogen makes up about 90 per cent of the giant planets.

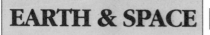

■ WHY WERE THE ASTEROIDS FORMED?

The asteroids consist of countless thousands of tiny planets left over from the Solar System's early history, when the Sun and planets were being formed. Most of them can be found in the wide gap between the orbits of Mars and Jupiter.

In the early days of the Solar System, space must have been quite thick with bodies like these. Gradually, though, they collided with each other and combined together to form the major planets. The largest asteroid, Ceres, is 1000 kilometres across but most asteroids are quite small.

QUIZ 49

1 What is the Caspian Sea?
2 What is its total area?
3 Is the water salty?
4 Which is the world's largest freshwater lake?
5 How large is it?
6 Which is the world's highest lake?
7 Which is the world's highest navigable lake?
8 Which is the world's largest single cave?
9 Which is the largest cave system in the world?
10 Which is the deepest cave in the world?

■ WHY DO SO MANY COMETS APPEAR UNEXPECTEDLY?

Most comets take thousands or even millions of years to go round the Sun, and their orbits are so elongated or 'eccentric' that they travel far beyond Pluto.

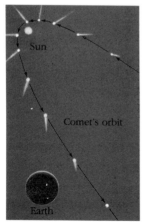

Very few become bright enough to see until they are as close as Mars. That is why some comets appear without warning every year. Not all comets are surprise visitors. The famous Halley's Comet, for example, has a period of 76 years and has been observed regularly since 239 BC. It will be seen again in 2062.

WHY DOES A COMET HAVE A TAIL?

A comet is a crumbly body of rock and ice only a few kilometres across. When it passes near the Sun and becomes hot, the ice turns into gas, and dusty fragments are thrown out into space. Clouds of particles flying out from the Sun (the solar wind) push back this gas and dust to form the comet's tail.

The finest tails are formed by comets that have passed the Sun only a few times. These can be millions of kilometres long, but are also very thin. In 1910, for example, the Earth passed harmlessly through the tail of Halley's Comet.

WHY DO ECLIPSES OF THE SUN OCCUR?

The Sun is about 400 times the diameter of the Moon, but it is also 400 times as far away from the Earth. This means that both bodies look about the same size in the sky when seen from Earth.

If the Moon passes in front of the Sun, it can block out the brilliant disc, so that the faint surrounding 'corona' can be seen. The beautiful corona can only be seen at New Moon, during a total eclipse.

QUIZ 50

1 What is the rock called which produces columns in caves?

2 In what direction does a stalactite grow?

3 What is a stalagmite?

4 Where are stalactites and stalagmites found?

5 What does sand mainly consist of?

6 What shape are desert sand grains?

7 If all the world's ice melted where would there be new land?

8 If all the ice melted, by how much would sea-level rise?

9 If all the ice melted, what would happen to London, Helsinki and Rome?

■ WHY DO METEORS OCCUR?

A meteor is a streak of light high up in the atmosphere. It occurs when a tiny solid object plunges through the air at a speed of many kilometres per second. The body is burned up by friction, leaving a white hot trail.

Before entering the Earth's atmosphere, those bodies are called 'meteoroids'. They orbit the sun like planets, some on their own, others in long swarms. If the Earth's orbit passes through one of these meteor swarms, a meteor shower is seen.

■ WHY MUST YOU NEVER LOOK AT THE SUN?

The surface of the Sun is about four times as hot as a furnace. The lens or cornea of your eye acts like a burning glass. If you look straight at the Sun, the lens would be destroyed for life.

Some people suggest looking at the Sun through smoked glass. Don't! The Sun may look dim, but the dangerous heat rays can pass through. Whenever there is an eclipse of the Sun, some people are blinded because they take foolish risks of this sort. To observe the Sun, you should project its image through binoculars or a telescope on to a sheet of white card held by a frame. Sunspots and other solar features can then be seen easily and safely or carefully studied by a group of people together.

QUIZ 51

1 What is artesian water?
2 Where does the name come from?
3 Where are the porous rocks found in an artesian basin?
4 What is the water-bearing layer called?
5 Where is the world's largest artesian basin?
6 How do people cause semi-desert areas to become deserts?
7 What is the soil like in semi-desert areas?
8 Is the climate always bad?
9 When was the 'dust bowl' in America?
10 Where in America was the most damaged area?

WHY DOES THE SUN KEEP SHINING?

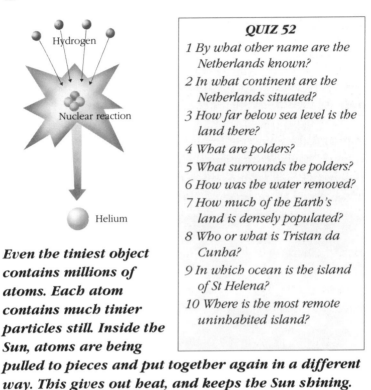

Hydrogen

Nuclear reaction

Helium

QUIZ 52

1 *By what other name are the Netherlands known?*

2 *In what continent are the Netherlands situated?*

3 *How far below sea level is the land there?*

4 *What are polders?*

5 *What surrounds the polders?*

6 *How was the water removed?*

7 *How much of the Earth's land is densely populated?*

8 *Who or what is Tristan da Cunha?*

9 *In which ocean is the island of St Helena?*

10 *Where is the most remote uninhabited island?*

Even the tiniest object contains millions of atoms. Each atom contains much tinier particles still. Inside the Sun, atoms are being pulled to pieces and put together again in a different way. This gives out heat, and keeps the Sun shining.

The Sun is made up of 90 per cent hydrogen atoms, about nine per cent helium atoms and one per cent other elements such as oxygen and nitrogen. In its centre hydrogen atoms are reassembled as helium atoms, giving out a burst of energy.

WHY IS THE SETTING SUN RED?

The Earth's atmosphere is like a pale red filter, and makes the light coming from space turn reddish.

But an object which is very low in the sky has to shine through much more air than one high in the sky. This means that its light passes through more of this red filter, and its tint is deeper. This is the cause of the 'red' evening sky.

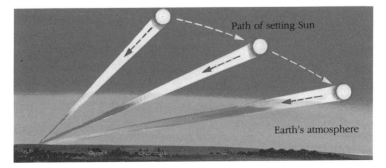

Path of setting Sun

Earth's atmosphere

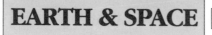

EARTH & SPACE

■ *HOW BIG IS THE SUN?*

The Sun measures 1,392,530 kilometres across, or 109 times the diameter of the Earth. Over a million Earths could be squashed into the Sun's globe. If the Sun were the size of a football, the Earth would be only two millimetres across.

Although the Sun is enormous compared with the planets, it is much smaller than many stars. The bright reddish star Betelgeuse in the constellation of Orion is larger than the orbit of the planet Mars, or about 300 times the Sun's diameter.

QUIZ 53

1 *Which continent has no permanent population?*

2 *Which is the most sparsely populated country?*

3 *Of which European country is Bouvet Island a dependency?*

4 *What is unusual about Lake Volta?*

5 *Where is the Akosombo Dam?*

6 *What does the Akosombo Dam produce?*

7 *Which reservoir holds the greatest volume of water?*

8 *Which is the largest modern quarry?*

9 *What do they mine for at this quarry?*

10 *What is the 'Big Hole' of Kimberley?*

■ *WHAT IS THE SUN'S CORONA?*

The corona is often called the Sun's atmosphere, but it is not at all like our own atmosphere. It has a temperature of a million degrees centigrade, and is a million times thinner than air.

The brilliance of the Sun hides it from view except during a total eclipse. During an eclipse, the corona seems to extend for one or two Sun-diameters into space.

WHAT IS THE MILKY WAY?

If the night is very clear and there is no Moon, a hazy band of light can be seen running through some of the constellations. This band is caused by distant stars, which cannot be seen separately with the naked eye.

The Milky Way is the proof, to the naked eye, of the shape of the Galaxy in which the Sun is located. If the Galaxy were spherical in shape, we should see distant, faint stars in all directions in the sky. The Milky Way effect suggests that the Galaxy must be flattened in form, like many other galaxies that can be observed with powerful telescopes.

WHICH IS THE NEAREST GALAXY TO OUR OWN?

Our Galaxy's closest neighbour is the Large Magellanic Cloud, which is about 150,000 light-years away. It is only one-third the diameter of our Galaxy, and contains only a tenth as many stars. The Small Magellanic Cloud is about 190,000 light-years away.

The nearest spiral galaxy like our own is the Andromeda galaxy, over two million light-years away. Like the Magellanic Clouds, it can be seen with the naked eye.

QUIZ 54

1 What is acid rain?
2 What will acid rain do to limestone?
3 Which cereal provides food for more people than any other?
4 Where is rice the basic food crop?
5 What climate and conditions does rice need to grow?
6 Why are rice fields irrigated?
7 What is cotton thread made from?
8 What is the cotton seed pod called?
9 Where was cotton a major crop?
10 How is it possible to tell when a cotton boll is ripe?

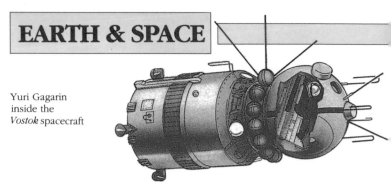

EARTH & SPACE

Yuri Gagarin
inside the
Vostok spacecraft

WHEN DID THE FIRST MAN FLY INTO SPACE?

The Soviet cosmonaut Yuri Gagarin made the first orbit of the Earth on 12 April 1961 in a Vostok spacecraft. The trip lasted 108 minutes, and landed within ten kilometres of the planned descent point.

The first orbit by an American was made by John Glenn in a *Mercury* spacecraft on 20 February 1962. Glenn was not the first American in space, for Alan Shepard had made a 'space-hop' on 5 May 1961. He reached an altitude of about 180 kilometres before returning to Earth. On 6 August the Soviet cosmonaut Herman Titov made 17 orbits of the Earth.

WHEN WAS THE FIRST ROCKET-PROPELLED VEHICLE LAUNCHED?

Rockets in the form of fireworks have been known for centuries but the first flight of a true rocket vehicle took place on 16 March 1926.

It was built and launched by an American, Robert Hutchings Goddard. His rocket rose about 60 metres into the air! Goddard's rocket was fuelled by petrol and liquid oxygen. He was interested in exploring the upper atmosphere,but also realized that by using two or three step rockets, which fire in succession, it would be possible to escape into space.

The first rocket to reach interplanetary space was a two-stage vehicle fired to a height of 400 kilometres from New Mexico in 1949.

QUIZ 55

1 What is tea?
2 In what kind of climate does it grow?
3 At what altitude does tea thrive best?
4 Where did tea first come from?
5 Where were plantations made later on?
6 Where does the milky fluid called latex come from?
7 Where is the rubber tree found originally?
8 How was it introduced to South-East Asia?
9 How is latex obtained from a rubber tree?
10 Does all rubber come from the rubber tree?

WHEN DID THE SPACE SHUTTLE MAKE ITS FIRST FLIGHT?

The first Space Shuttle launch took place on 12 April 1981, using the vehicle Columbia. *A second shuttle,* Challenger, *made its maiden flight on 4 April 1984.*

Since then both shuttles have been used for further flights. In the hands of commander John Young and pilot Robert Crippen, *Columbia* made 36 orbits of the Earth during a 54-hour stay in space on its first voyage.

> **QUIZ 56**
> 1 What is maize?
> 2 Where did it originate?
> 3 How did North American Indians regard maize?
> 4 How important was 'Indian corn' to the settlers in North America?
> 5 How is maize now used?
> 6 Where did cocoa originate?
> 7 Who were the earliest drinkers of cocoa?
> 8 Where does the cacao plant thrive?
> 9 How long is a cocoa pod?
> 10 How many cocoa beans are there in a pod?

WHEN DID THE FIRST SPACECRAFT LAND ON ANOTHER WORLD?

Soviet spacecraft made the first direct landings on the Moon on 13 September 1959. Venera 3 *reached Venus in March 1966; and* Mars 2 *landed on Mars in November 1971.*

The first American craft to reach another world was *Ranger 7*, which struck the Moon on 31 July 1964. The first spacecraft to land people on the Moon was *Apollo 11*, on 16 July 1969. The photograph shows astronaut Buzz Aldrin on the Moon's surface. *Venera 4*, which landed on Venus on 18 October 1967, was the first probe to send back information from the surface of another planet.

Pulsar

Beam from pulsar

Earth

■ WHAT IS A PULSAR?

After a supernova explosion, all that is left of a star is a very hot ball of matter a few kilometres across, spinning at a tremendous rate. It sends out a beam of light that it seems to 'pulse' on and off. It is called a pulsar.

These remains are the shrunken core of the original star, at a temperature of millions of degrees. One of the strongest pulsars is the star at the centre of the Crab Nebula, which rotates 30 times a second. The fastest known pulsar, however, rotates 642 times a second.

QUIZ 57

1. Do we know why an Ice Age begins?
2. When was the last Ice Age on Earth?
3. What are the periods of ice advances called?
4. When was the 'Little Ice Age', when winters were colder than they are today?
5. By what process are all sand grains formed?
6. What is the most common mineral in sand?
7. What speed does the wind reach during a sandstorm?
8. Where would you be if you were caught in an avalanche?
9. What is the worst time of year for an avalanche?

■ WHAT ARE NOVAE AND SUPERNOVAE?

Both of these objects are exploding stars, which erupt almost overnight. Several novae occur in our Galaxy every year, and some can be seen with the naked eye. Supernovae are more rare.

All novae seem to be close binary stars. The outburst, which can raise the brightness of the binary by 10,000 times, is caused by gas from one star pouring on to its companion. A supernova is a single star several times more massive than the Sun. It becomes so hot inside that the outer layers cannot hold in the radiation. For a few days, it sends out as much energy as a whole galaxy of thousands of millions of stars. A supernova was seen in the Large Magellanic Cloud in 1987.

WHAT IS THE AGE OF THE UNIVERSE?

The galaxies in the universe appear to be expanding away from each other. If we work backwards, we find that they were close together between 15,000 and 20,000 million years ago. Is this when the universe began?

Most astronomers agree that the galaxies are flying away from some explosion that 'created' the universe. But it is impossible to say why this explosion, or 'Big Bang', occurred.

After the 'Bang', matter was formed in the tremendous heat, and galaxies were created.

HOW WILL THE UNIVERSE END?

Nobody knows – yet. The galaxies may go on flying apart for ever. However, they might begin to slow down, come to a halt and then fly inwards pulled by gravity to collide in the 'Big Crunch'. At the moment astronomers cannot make sufficiently accurate observations to decide.

The future of the universe depends upon the amount of material it contains. The greater the amount of material, the more powerful is the gravitational force trying to pull the galaxies back together. It is similar to launching a spacecraft. The more massive the planet, the faster the spacecraft must move to escape into space.

QUIZ 58

1 Where are rain forests found?
2 Where is the world's largest rain forest?
3 Are there many different kinds of trees in the rain forest?
4 How high do rain forest trees grow?
5 What happens if the rain forest is cut down?
6 How much of the rainforest is destroyed every minute?
7 At this rate, when will all the rain forests in the world have been destroyed?
8 How many of the world's species depend on these forests to survive?

EARTH & SPACE

QUIZ 1

1 Towers, columns and castle-like masses.
2 Yes, quite natural.
3 Yes.
4 A number do.
5 Mount Kilimanjaro; the peaks of the Andes.
6 5894 metres.
7 No. It is slightly flattened at the Poles.
8 No, it is not.
9 40,075.03 kilometres.
10 12,756.28 kilometres.

QUIZ 2

1 Oil, natural gas and coal.
2 The remains of tiny plants and animals.
3 Porous.
4 Impervious.
5 Millions of years ago.
6 The remains of trees and plants.
7 layer of coal in rock.
8 About 360 million years old.
9 The Donbas coalfield, the Ukraine.

QUIZ 3

1 Very hot, molten rock.
2 The crust, the mantle, the outer and inner core.
3 The study of earthquakes.
4 Three kinds.
5 Primary, secondary and long.
6 Primary waves.
7 China, in 1976.
8 250,000.
9 The strength of an earthquake.
10 A severe earthquake.

QUIZ 4

1 The science of measuring the Earth.
2 Measuring long distances very accurately.
3 He measured the Earth's circumference.
4 The founder of modern geology.
5 Igneous, sedimentary and metamorphic.
6 'Fire-formed'.
7 Molten material which cooled down.
8 Made from sediments.
9 'Transformed'.

QUIZ 5

1 They would fly off into space.
2 Venus – it is closer to the Sun.
3 Anti-clockwise.
4 Anti-clockwise.
5 No.
6 Hydrogen, oxygen and nitrogen.
7 No – only on Earth.
8 As a shield from the Sun's dangerous rays.

QUIZ 6

1 4.3 light years.
2 No, it would be invisible.
3 300,000 kilometres per second.
4 9.5 million million kilometres.
5 Not for certain.
6 Alpha Centauri.
7 Sirius, also known as the Dog Star.
8 Free fall.
9 In the spacecraft.
10 A star.

QUIZ 7

1 A dark body orbiting a star.
2 By the starlight it reflects.
3 A satellite of a planet.
4 Nine.
5 Mercury and Venus.

6 Jupiter has sixteen.

7 Phobos and Deimos.

8 Ganymede.

9 Saturn.

10 Yes.

QUIZ 8

1 Waxing.

2 It shrinks to invisibility.

3 No.

4 4500 million years.

5 29 days.

6 Smaller bodies, a few kilometres across, collided with the moon.

7 Because there is no erosion on the Moon.

8 Yes, there once were.

9 Diana.

QUIZ 9

1 Towards the Earth.

2 About two days after New Moon.

3 It lies almost between the Earth and the Sun.

4 384,000 kilometres.

5 No.

6 Because there is no atmosphere to carry noise.

7 Higher than boiling water.

8 There are no signs of life.

9 H.G. Wells.

QUIZ 10

1 Mars

2 Iron

3 A kind of rust!

4 There is a permanent haze of red dust.

5 Because Martian winds raise thick clouds of dust.

6 Grand Canyon, USA.

7 Jupiter.

8 In 9 hours, 50 minutes.

9 In 10 hours, 16 minutes.

10 A perfect sphere.

QUIZ 11

1 Sulphuric acid.

2 117 days.

3 Yes, like a thick blanket.

4 480°C.

5 108.2 million kilometres.

6 Mercury.

7 88 days.

8 4880 kilometres.

9 None!

10 Never very clearly.

QUIZ 12

1 Many small pieces of rock and ice.

2 Christian Huygens in 1659.

3 About 22 times the diameter of the Earth.

4 A few kilometres across.

5 From a huge cloud of gas and tiny solid particles.

6 4600 million years ago.

7 Yes, much stronger than the Earth's.

8 Hydrogen.

9 On Jupiter.

QUIZ 13

1 Thousands of tiny planets.

2 Between the orbits of Mars and Jupiter.

3 Ceres.

4 1000 kilometres across.

5 270 kilometres across.

6 76 years.

7 1986.

8 Gas and dust.

9 1976.

10 Comet Enke.

QUIZ 14

1 A crumbly body of rock and ice.

2 16 x 8 kilometres.

3 It warms up and gives off a tail of gas.

4 Millions of kilometres long.

5 *A streak of light in the atmosphere.*

6 *Smaller than a marble.*

7 *A tiny lump of rock called a meteroid.*

8 *The Perseids.*

9 *Wilkes Land, Antarctica.*

QUIZ 15

1 *6000° C.*

2 *Yes! The lens of your eye acts like a burning glass.*

3 *Your lens would be burnt.*

4 *Dangerous heat rays can pass through.*

5 *Only for use for projecting the Sun's image on to a card.*

6 *1,392,500 kilometres.*

7 *It is 400 times bigger, but 400 times further away.*

8 *It blocks out the Sun.*

9 *The surrounding glare.*

QUIZ 16

1 *The Earth's atmosphere acts like a pale red filter.*

2 *About 28 times Earth's gravity.*

3 *Hydrogen.*

4 *15,000,000 ° C.*

5 *They are being broken down and reassembled as helium atoms.*

6 *Four.*

7 *Thousands of millions of years.*

8 *A very large star, bigger than the Sun.*

9 *A Blue Giant.*

QUIZ 17

1 *About 100,000 million.*

2 *Some are hotter, some cooler.*

3 *It is the centre of our Solar System.*

4 *No, it is very ordinary.*

5 *Yes.*

6 *Red dwarfs.*

7 *The corona.*

8 *In 585 BC, between Lydia and Medea.*

9 *During a total eclipse.*

10 *The photosphere.*

QUIZ 18

1 *A hazy band of light in the night sky.*

2 *Distant stars.*

3 *The shape of the Galaxy in which the Sun is located.*

4 *No, flattened in form.*

5 *Yes, through powerful telescopes.*

6 *The galaxy nearest our own.*

7 *150,000 light-years.*

8 *Andromeda.*

9 *About 30.*

QUIZ 19

1 *Robert Hutchings Goddard.*

2 *By petrol and liquid oxygen.*

3 *The first direct landing on the Moon.*

4 Luna 2 *landed.*

5 Venera 3 *on 1 March 1966.*

6 Ranger 7 *which struck the Moon 31 July 1964.*

7 *Soviet craft* Luna 9 *on 3 February 1966.*

8 *The first American craft to make a 'soft' landing.*

QUIZ 20

1 *Soviet cosmonaut Yuri Gagarin.*

2 *The first orbit of the Earth was made.*

3 *Laika, a Soviet dog.*

4 *Alan Shepard.*

5 *12 US Astronauts.*

6 *Soviet cosmonaut Herman Titov.*

7 Columbia.

8 *Helen Sharman.*

9 Challenger *flew on 4 April 1983.*

QUIZ 21

1 *3850 million years old.*
2 *4600 million years old.*
3 *510,065,600 square kilometres.*
4 *By studying the decay of radioactive elements.*
5 *3850 million years ago.*
6 *Yes, 450 million years ago.*
7 *A supercontinent.*
8 *200 million years ago.*
9 *Near the South Pole.*
10 *Diagonally across South America.*

QUIZ 22

1 *Europe, Asia and Africa*
2 *North and South America*
3 *Over the last 150 million years.*
4 *Panthalassa.*
5 *Yes.*
6 *Because the Alps are younger.*
7 *25 million years ago.*
8 *From the movement of continents after the break-up of Pangaea.*

QUIZ 23

1 *It was a dry valley.*
2 *Salt, hundreds of metres thick.*
3 *Very hot and dry.*
4 *Very few.*
5 *Round.*
6 *As a sphere.*
7 *They studied the Earth and Moon during eclipses.*
8 *The spherical shape.*

QUIZ 24

1 *1270.*
2 *Louix IX of France.*

3 *By keeping close to land or drifting with currents.*
4 *Gar-Sur, near Babylon.*
5 *From about 2300 BC.*
6 *Mountains and rivers in Babylonia.*
7 *The Egyptians and Greeks.*
8 *To record land boundaries.*
9 *The ancient Greeks.*

QUIZ 25

1 *Gerardus Mercator.*
2 *They were drawn by hand.*
3 *One was produced in 1477.*
4 *Abraham Ortelius in 1570.*
5 *After the Greek god Atlas.*
6 *Gaspard Felix Tournachon.*
7 *From a balloon.*
8 *Over Paris in 1858.*
9 *To help with map-making.*
10 *During World War I.*

QUIZ 26

1 *No, some crops put goodness back.*
2 *With manures and fertilizers.*
3 *The field is being rested for a year.*
4 *For 2000 years.*
5 *About 3000 BC.*
6 *In India.*
7 *Sugar.*
8 *Christopher Columbus in 1493.*
9 *The orange.*

QUIZ 27

1 *65 million years ago.*
2 *For 130 million years.*
3 *No, no one is sure.*
4 *Yes, flying and sea reptiles.*
5 *Six metres tall, with jaws almost two metres long!*
6 *Yes – the Stegosaurus had a brain the size of a plum.*
7 *For information about conditions in the past.*

8 Plant and animal fossils from a variety of places.

QUIZ 28
1 Near Sunderland.
2 Yes, but they are very few.
3 The Antarctic was once much warmer.
4 Yes, formed from fossil plants.
5 A relatively thin layer on the surface.
6 By convection currents inside the Earth.
7 10 million gallons.
8 Small seas; shallow seas.

QUIZ 29
1 Molten rock
2 From the Earth's mantle.
3 Magma.
4 Under the crust of the Earth.
5 1783.
6 Molten rock, and gases.
7 Near the edges of the Earth's crustal plates.
8 Around 1000.

QUIZ 30
1 In volcanic areas.
2 No.
3 Underground water is heated under pressure.
4 A pressure cooker.
5 It gets colder.
6 150 million kilometres.
7 The Earth.
8 By shortwave radiation.
9 The Waimangu geyser, New Zealand.
10 Yellowstone Park, USA.

QUIZ 31
1 From minerals washed into the sea.
2 About 85 per cent.
3 Where there is a lot of evaporation.
4 The Dead Sea.
5 The Baltic Sea.
6 The chemical name for salt.
7 The Moon's gravity.
8 Twice in 25 hours.
9 They occur about one hour later every day.
10 27 and one-third days.

QUIZ 32
1 Cirrostratus.
2 Yes.
3 Warm air can hold more water vapour than cold air.
4 It cannot hold so much water vapour.
5 Cumulus cloud.
6 The droplets fall as rain.
7 Clouds, at ground level.
8 A huge spark of electricity.
9 The Tropics.

QUIZ 33
1 Trees, and high buildings.
2 Because they are tall, and often damp.
3 With a downward leader stroke.
4 With a lightning conductor.
5 Strips of copper.
6 Up to 1500 kilometres a second.
7 A piece of ice.
8 Layers upon layer of ice.
9 In temperate or tropical areas.
10 1.02 kg.

QUIZ 34
1 Ice crystals clinging together.
2 No.
3 From condensed water vapour.
4 Other forms of hurricane.
5 A spiralling, very fast wind.
6 Up to 350 kilometres per hour.

7 400 kilometres across.

8 It is slightly bent.

9 The colours are separated out to form the rainbow.

10 Seven.

QUIZ 35

1 A delta.

2 From the shape of the Greek letter 'delta'.

3 By deposits left by the river.

4 On the Ganges.

5 The Rhône.

6 Yes, a number do.

7 The area becomes an almost flat plain.

8 Australia.

9 Evaporation.

10 North America.

QUIZ 36

1 Like a great river of ice.

2 In very cold climates.

3 Antarctica.

4 Yes, under its own weight.

5 The last Ice Age.

6 Five, in the last two million years.

7 Humus, bacteria and minerals.

8 A permeable rock.

9 Impermeable.

10 They provide minerals.

QUIZ 37

1 About one fifth.

2 Strong and hot.

3 Loose sand can be driven along by the wind.

4 Because there is less rain.

5 Strong winds move sand further out.

6 Yes, new material is being added.

7 From volcanoes.

8 Material is being lost at the junction of certain plates.

9 Yes.

QUIZ 38

1 In Western California.

2 The Pacific coast.

3 North-westwards.

4 Anti-clockwise.

5 Africa.

6 6500 kilometres.

7 Between 30 and 60 kilometres.

8 A piece of gneiss from Greenland.

9 3800 billion years.

QUIZ 39

1 In the Colorado Desert.

2 1600 million years.

3 In deep mines.

4 Yes, in factories.

5 Over 1400°C.

6 Millions of years ago.

7 In mineral veins in rocks.

8 Alaska, California and the Andes.

9 To find grains of gold.

10 In the Chilean Andes.

QUIZ 40

1 The highest mountain range on land.

2 Mount Everest.

3 8848 metres high.

4 Sir George Everest, former Surveyor-General of India.

5 The Andes of South America.

6 The Andes.

7 Ojos del Salada, 6885m.

8 Mauna Loa, on Hawaii.

9 4170 metres .

10 About every 3$^{1}/_{2}$ years.

QUIZ 41

1 Southern Italy.

2 Vesuvius erupted.

3 It was buried in ash.

4 About 2000.

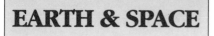

5 Details of Roman life.
6 A ring of fiery volcanic activity.
7 About 850.
8 Yes, in the western USA and Alaska.
9 A chain of volcanic islands.
10 Yes, in Kamchatka and Japan.

QUIZ 42
1 At Al'Aziziyah in Libya.
2 Death Valley – 56.7°C recorded in 1913.
3 The eastern Sahara.
4 4300 hours.
5 Antarctica.
6 In 1983, -89.2°C in Antarctica.
7 Verkhoyansk in Siberia.
8 Small crystals of ice.
9 When the temperature is low enough for water vapour to condense as ice.

QUIZ 43
1 Cherrapunji, in India.
2 26,461 millimetres.
3 Mt Wai'-ale'-ale, Hawaii.
4 The Atacama Desert in northern Chile.
5 400 years.
6 Yes. Large parts of Central Asia are without much rain.
7 The Lambert-Fisher Ice Passage.
8 515 kilometres.
9 Petermanns Glacier.
10 40 kilometres.

QUIZ 44
1 10 per cent.
2 87 per cent.
3 12.5 per cent.
4 Permanently frozen ground.
5 Beneath permanent ice and snow.
6 In Siberia.
7 Over 31,000 square kilometres.
8 From Greenland.
9 167 metres above the water.
10 50 metres above the sea.

QUIZ 45
1 The West Wind Drift.
2 In the Antarctic.
3 By strong westerly winds.
4 The Gulf of Mexico.
5 The Weddell Sea, Antarctica.
6 Early sailors.
7 About 5° north of the Equator.
8 A warm ocean current.
9 100 kilometres wide.
10 Nakwakto Rapids, Canada.

QUIZ 46
1 10,900 metres deep.
2 In 1951.
3 Yes, the bathyscaphe Trieste descended in 1960.
4 The Dead Sea.
5 On the borders of Israel and Jordan.
6 It has no exit.
7 A sea studded with islands.
8 South-East Asia.
9 Over 13,000.
10 Hudson Bay, Canada.

QUIZ 47
1 Coral.
2 2027 kilometres long.
3 Off the north-east coast of Australia.
4 Kwajalein, the Marshall Islands.
5 Narrow inlets of the sea.
6 A U-shaped valley.
7 Norway.
8 183 kilometres long.
9 Greenland, Iceland, Canada, Alaska, New Zealand and

Chile.

10 El Cañon de Colca, Peru.

QUIZ 48

1 The Nile

2 6448 kilometres long.

3 The Amazon.

4 The Mississippi-Missouri.

5 180,000 cubic m/s.

6 In Venezuela.

7 979 metres.

8 In Natal, South Africa.

9 The Hwang-ho River, in China.

10 Around 900,000 people.

QUIZ 49

1 The world's largest lake.

2 371,800 square kilometres.

3 Yes, very salty.

4 Lake Superior.

5 82,103 square kilometres.

6 A glacial lake near Mount Everest.

7 Lake Titicaca, Peru.

8 Sarawak Chamber, Sarawak.

9 The Mammoth Cave National Park, Kentucky.

10 The Gouffre Jean Bernard Cave, French Alps.

QUIZ 50

1 Dripstone.

2 Down.

3 Columns of dripstone rising from the floor.

4 In limestone caves.

5 Mostly quartz.

6 Quite rounded.

7 In the Arctic and Antarctic.

8 65 metres.

9 The cities would be drowned.

QUIZ 51

1 Underground water which rises to the surface under natural pressure.

2 From Artois in France.

3 Sandwiched between impervious layers.

4 An aquifer.

5 The Great Artesian Basin of Australia.

6 By poor farming methods and mismanagement.

7 Fragile.

8 No. There are good years.

9 The 1930s.

10 The Southern Great Plains.

QUIZ 52

1 Holland.

2 Europe.

3 Most is below 30 metres.

4 Areas of reclaimed land.

5 Dykes and ditches.

6 Formerly by wind pumps, but now by diesel pumps.

7 Only a fifth.

8 A remote island in the South Atlantic.

9 The Atlantic.

10 Bouvet Island, S Atlantic.

QUIZ 53

1 Antarctica

2 Greenland.

3 Norway.

4 It is a huge artificial lake.

5 On the River Volta in Ghana.

6 Hydro-electric power.

7 The Bratsk Reservoir in south-east Siberia.

8 Bingham Canyon Mine, in Utah, USA.

9 Copper.

10 An old diamond mine about 500 metres across.

QUIZ 54

1 Rain which has absorbed waste gases.

2 It will dissolve it.

3 Rice.

4 Much of Asia.
5 Hot weather and plenty of water.
6 To provide necessary water.
7 A fibre from the cotton plant.
8 A cotton boll.
9 In south-eastern USA.
10 It bursts open.

QUIZ 55

1 The crushed leaves of an evergreen bush.
2 In hot, damp climates.
3 At quite high altitudes.
4 From China.
5 In Indonesia, Sri Lanka and India.
6 The rubber tree.
7 The Amazon rain forest.
8 Via the Botanical Gardens at Kew, England!
9 By cutting the bark.
10 No.

QUIZ 56

1 A cereal crop
2 In America
3 As an important food crop.
4 It was often a 'life-saver' for them!

5 As cattle food, and also for flour.
6 In Central America.
7 The Aztecs.
8 In hot, wet forested areas.
9 15-35 centimetres long.
10 30-40 beans.

QUIZ 57

1 No.
2 10,000 years ago.
3 Glacials.
4 1550–1880.
5 They are weathered out of rocks.
6 Quartz.
7 About 16 kilometres per hour.
8 On a high, snowy mountain.
9 Late winter.

QUIZ 58

1 In Equatorial areas.
2 In the Amazon forest.
3 Yes – 3000 species in the forests of Indonesia alone.
4 About 45 metres.
5 Desert is created.
6 40 hectares.
7 2025 AD.
8 About half the world's species.

INDEX